A New Owner's
Guide to
AIREDALE TERRIERS

JG-160

Overleaf: Airedale Terrier photographed by Paulette Braun.

Opposite Page: Airedale Terrier photographed by Isabelle Francais.

The Publisher wishes to acknowledge the following owners of the dogs in this book, including: David and Dianne Barclay, Dionys Briggs, Brisline Airedales, Sarah Coleman Brock, Judy Brown, Carolyn Campbell, Steve and Mary Clark, Tim and Gail Collins, Samantha Curran, June Dutcher, Mary Evans, Barbara Fakkema, Carole Bullwinkle Foucrault, Bruck and Glenna Holmberg, Mary Johnson, Pia Lundberg, Mr. and Mrs. Charles Marck, Georgia McRae, Helen J. Piperis, Allan Des Roches, Jack and Mary Sanderson, Anne Sorraghan, Karen Wigley-Morrison.

Photographers: Ashbey Photography, Backstage Photo, Paulette Braun, Dionys Briggs, Callea Photo, Cook Photo, Dog Ads, Isabelle Francais, Ludwig Photos, Debbie Melmon, Duff Munson, Don Porter, Ron Reagan, George Shagawat, Robert Smith, The Standard Image, Judith Strom, Karen Taylor, Missy Yuhl

The author acknowledges the contribution of Judy Iby to the following chapters: Health Care, Sport of Purebred Dogs, Identification and Finding the Lost Dog, Traveling with Your Dog, and Behavior and Canine Communication.

Distributed in the UNITED STATES to the Pet Trade by T.F.H. Publications, Inc., 1 TFH Plaza, Neptune City, NJ 07753; on the Internet at www.tfh.com; in CANADA by Rolf C. Hagen Inc., 3225 Sartelon St., Montreal, Quebec H4R 1E8; Pet Trade by H & L Pet Supplies Inc., 27 Kingston Crescent, Kitchener, Ontario N2B 2T6; in ENGLAND by T.F.H. Publications, PO Box 74, Havant PO9 5TT; in AUSTRALIA AND THE SOUTH PACIFIC by T.F.H. (Australia), Pty. Ltd., Box 149, Brookvale 2100 N.S.W., Australia; in NEW ZEALAND by Brooklands Aquarium Ltd., 5 McGiven Drive, New Plymouth, RD1 New Zealand; in SOUTH AFRICA by Rolf C. Hagen S.A. (PTY.) LTD., P.O. Box 201199, Durban North 4016, South Africa; in JAPAN by T.F.H. Publications. Published by T.F.H. Publications, Inc.

MANUFACTURED IN THE
UNITED STATES OF AMERICA
BY T.F.H. PUBLICATIONS, INC.

A New Owner's Guide to
AIREDALE TERRIERS

BETTY-ANNE STENMARK

Contents

2000 Edition

Regular exercise is important to your Airedale's physical health and mental well-being.

Long-legged terriers like the Airedale were used to hunt prey above ground.

The Airedale Terrier is an athletic and versatile dog.

With proper care and lots of love, your Airedale puppy can become a valued family member.

Who can resist an adorable Airedale puppy?

HISTORY and Origin of the Airedale Terrier

Terriers derive their name from the Latin word, *terra*, meaning earth. They were developed to go to ground after vermin, most often fox and badger, but also weasel, otter, rats, mice, and anything else that caught their eye. The first terriers were short-legged, with slightly crooked front legs that were ideally suited for their work underground, digging in and out of burrows. They were bold, brash, and tenacious, and impervious to pain and damage inflicted by their enemy, whatever it was.

The earliest recorded writings about terriers are from the 14th century by the poet, Gace de la Vigne, who wrote about an "earthe dogge." Messr. de la Vigne wrote, "He goes to earth with the good Terrier dog that they put in the burrow." Two centuries later, Dr. Johannes Caius (translated in English as Dr. John Keyes) wrote in his book, *De Canibus Britannicis,* about the "earthe dogge," referring to the aggressive nature of some small, hound-like dogs.

Because of their stature, long-legged terriers, like the Airedale, were used to hunt above ground— to chase, capture, and return to the hunters with their quarry.

While other earth dogs and Dachshunds came from Western Europe, most of the terrier family we know today has origins firmly rooted in the British Isles. These terriers are divided into two groups: the short-legged, go-to-ground breeds such as the Cairn, Dandie Dinmont, and West Highland White, and the long-legged class to which the Kerry Blue, Irish, Airedale, and others of their ilk belong. Because of their stature, long-legged terriers like the Airedale were used to hunt above ground, to chase, to capture, and to return with their freshly killed quarry dangling triumphantly from their mouths. The Airedale was a multi-purpose hunter, a true sporting terrier with a special affinity for water, gamely working water rats in the streams around the Aire River. No one can tell us which breeds were the progenitors of the Airedale with certainty, but some informed guesswork can be made. The now-extinct Old

English Terrier is mentioned as one of the forebearers of all of
the long-legged terriers. The Old English Terrier has had many
names, among them the Broken-coated Working Terrier,
Rough-coated Black-and-Tan Terrier, and Old English Black-and-
Tan Terrier, all of which could describe the Airedale we know
today. This early Old English Terrier was much smaller,
however, more the size of a Fox Terrier, and sometimes
smooth or woolly in coat. It came in varying colors, from
shades of red to grizzles and bluish grays, in addition to the
black-and-tan pattern.

The Otterhound is mentioned often by early scholars as
surely being behind the Airedale. In Vero Shaw's book, *The
Classic Encyclopedia of the Dog*, first published 1879-1881,
there is an etching of Mr. J. C. Carrick's Otterhound, "Lottery,"
born in 1876. The etching certainly adds credence to the
theory that the Otterhound is behind the Airedale. Lottery is of
an upright build with good bone and substance, covered in a
rough double-coat, with a long and balanced head. Comparing
Lottery to etchings of Airedale Jerry, whelped in England in
1888 and said to be the foundation sire of the modern Airedale,
there is more similarity than difference. Change the set-on of
both Lottery's tail and ears, dock the tail, and shorten the ears,
and Lottery could be a close relative of Airedale Jerry. The
Otterhound would also be beneficial for increasing the size.
Lottery's owner exhibited him at several shows and he was
highly regarded. His measurements were recorded; he was 24
inches at the shoulder and weighed 78 pounds.

Size was of concern to early Airedale fanciers. In 1902, a
report from the Airedale Terrier Club read, "...size is one, if not
the most important characteristic of the breed...and judges
shall consider undersized specimens of the breed as severely
handicapped when competing with dogs of standard weight
(at that time, 40-45 pounds)...and that any of the Club's judges
who, in the opinion of the Committee, shall give prizes or
otherwise push to the front dogs of small type, shall be at once
struck from the list of specialized specialist judges." Also,
"Judges ought to be particularly careful in not giving prizes to
animals too small in size and which are likely to resemble in
appearance the Irish or Welsh Terrier." It's interesting that
then, as now, fanciers were concerned with proper size, it
being one of the major differences between the Airedale and

his cousins, the more lightly built Irish Terrier and the smaller Welsh Terrier.

The other breed most often mentioned in the early history of the Airedale was the Bull Terrier. Whether the Bull Terrier was used before or after the Otterhound is up for discussion, but most authorities believe that the Bull Terrier was bred to the Old English Terrier to increase the boldness and tenacity so highly regarded by the terrier owners of the day. Whether used to go to ground or to chase and capture above ground, "gameness" was highly regarded and essential in a working terrier.

Early black-and-tan, broken-coated terriers were known by several names and reflected the area where these dogs were first known, the English-Scottish border country of Yorkshire. Vero Shaw's book talks about the old Yorkshire Waterside Terrier, while others refer to the Bingley Terrier, which no doubt refers to the town of Bingley, located in Yorkshire. Lore has it that a judge at a show in Bingley was so impressed with the large entry of Waterside Terriers before him that he said that such a popular and important breed

Originating in the British Isles, the Airedale possesses the tenacity and determination of his terrier ancestors. Arthur Airedale does what comes naturally on an Australian beach.

should have a better name than the Waterside Terrier. Since the show itself was known as the Airedale show, that name was given to the breed.

Today, we know that continuous selection for certain characteristics in just a few generations can change the entire look of a breed. This is how the early breeds were established. The breeder selected the dogs that were best for the purpose at hand, whether he was a sportsman using his terriers to accompany the hounds on a hunt after fox and badger through the Scottish border country or a factory worker using his dog for water rat or otter hunting in the waters of the Aire River region. The modern Airedale evolved through continued selection and was acknowledged by all lovers of the numerous terrier breeds as "The King of Terriers."

The first dog shows in England took place in the 1840s and were unregulated for almost two decades. The Keighly Agriculture Show, held in the Aire Valley in 1864, included a class for "Broken-haired Terriers" in which Waterside Terriers competed with Dandie Dinmonts, rough Fox Terriers, Bedlingtons, and Scottish Terriers. Regulation of shows began in 1873 with the formation of The Kennel

The Airedale is well-known for his abilities as a multi-purpose hunter and sporting dog. Airedales Rheece and Kate help herd sheep.

Selective breeding has allowed the Airedale to retain his gameness and reputation as a hardy, working terrier.

Club, and the first stud book was created, containing some 4,027 dogs. There were two classifications: sporting dogs, under which gun dogs and hounds were included, and non-sporting dogs, under which rough-coated terriers were listed. Six years later, the Waterside or Bingley Terriers were first mentioned by name by judge and author Hugh Dalziel in his critique of the entry after judging at Bingley. He wrote, "The class for Broken-haired Terriers, the Bingley Terrier par excellence—was an exceedingly good one." A year later, Mr. Dalziel compared the Bingley Terrier to the appearance of a giant Bedlington or Dandie Dinmont in his book, and wrote that they were "appearing to have a lot of hound blood." Other fanciers of the Broken-haired Terrier were outraged by his designation of the Bingley Terrier and thought they should be known as Airedale Terriers. The dogs continued to be shown under several different names, and it wasn't until 1886 that The Kennel Club conceded that the name would be Airedale.

It was two years later that the dog Aircdale Jerry, by Rattler and out of Bess, was born in England. He was to become the acknowledged foundation sire of the breed. Almost every line today in England and America can be traced back to this important dog. In F. M. Jowett's book, *The Complete Story of the Airedale Terrier*, published in 1913, he described Airedale Jerry as "a big, strong-boned dog with a long, typical head and a real hard, wiry coat, but overdone in ears."

Jerry's son, Ch. Cholmondeley Briar, was also described by Mr. Jowett. "He had a beautiful long, clean, typical head, with great power in front of the eyes, nice small ears, lovely neck, and clean, well-placed shoulders, with good, short, firm back and well-set, gaily carried tail. His bone and legs and feet were extraordinary, and as round and firm as an English Foxhound's, and being well covered with hair, gave him an appearance of immense strength. In color he was dense

The Airedale has a special affinity for the water and is an excellent retriever. Ron Sorraghan takes his eager Airedales, Bess and Cleo, for a dip.

black on his back with rich golden tan on his legs and quarters, and his coat was both straight and hard. He had any amount of substance, yet he was all Terrier, with nothing houndy or coarse about him. He was well up to standard weight..." This description of Briar would befit a quality Airedale today.

Proving once again that quality begets quality, 12 generations down from Airedale Jerry came the dog Eng/Am. Ch. Warland Ditto, from whom all great modern sires are said to descend. According to breed stalwart and author Gladys Brown Edwards in her 1978 book, *The Complete Airedale Terrier*, "all great modern sires...are strongly linebred to Ditto." This dog had a profound effect on both English and American bloodlines through several branches. Defined by Mrs. Edwards, it was found that "modern English Champions are preponderantly of the English Ch. Clee Courtier (1925) branch of the Warland Whatnot line from Ditto, just as in the United States, but are divided almost equally between Eng. Ch.

12

The Airedale Terrier was shown under many different names, including Broken-haired and Rough-coated Terrier, until 1886. Ch. Finlair Tiger of Stone Ridge, one of the top-winning Airedales of all time.

Matador Mandarin (1929) and Walnut King Nobbler (1930)."

It cannot be disputed that England has continued to have a major influence on American Airedales. Four generations down from Ditto off the Mandarin branch was Eng. Ch. Son of Merrijak, who in turn sired Ch. Bengal Bahadur of Harham (1950),

imported by Harold Florsheim of Harham Airedales in Chicago,
Illinois from the Bengal Airedale kennels of Mrs. Mollie
Harmsworth in England. Bahadur enjoyed considerable success
in the show ring and also as a sire, producing the top winner
and producer, Am/Can. Ch. Aireline Star Monarch, whelped in
1951 and co-bred by Charles Ryan and Percy Roberts.

Eight generations down from Ditto came the great import
Ch. Bengal Sabu, under the sponsorship of Mr. Florsheim.
Imported in 1959 at one year of age, he left three litters in
England and became a top winner in America in the 1960s.
Some deemed him "the Sire of the Sixties." In Dan
Kiedrowski's treatise, *The King of Terriers—An Overview*
(1980), Mr. Kiedrowski summarizes the great British breeders,
their dogs, the exports, and their influence in America. Mr.
Kiedrowski wrote this about Sabu's appearance at Montgomery
County Kennel Club in 1969, which sums up beautifully what
Sabu meant as an Airedale. "Perhaps the most spontaneously
joyous happening of the day was the entrance of the lone
veteran, Ch. Bengal Sabu...majestically surveying his
surroundings before entering the ring, kicking up a minor sand
storm, and then proudly trotting around the ring as if this
space was his alone...and on this day it was! How grand he
looked, and how proud Mollie Harmsworth must have felt as
she took over the lead to show her now famous homebred in
breed competition. Proud, too, were his owners, Barbara
Strebeigh (Birchrun) and Tuck Dell (Dellaire). It was like the
largest of all possible family reunions...so many of the dogs
represented on this day carrying his majestic blood (Best of
Breed was his great-great-great-grandson, Eng/Am. Ch. Jokyl
Superman). The ringside applause that seemed to never stop,
quickly brought viewers from other breed rings, asking, 'who
is it?' It was the great Sabu...nothing more had to be said."

For those of you not familiar with the Montgomery County
Kennel Club show, held in Pennsylvania each October, it is
simply the best all-terrier show in the world, and a win there
means everything to a diehard terrier devotee.

I have purposely not recounted the endless records amassed
by the famous Airedales in America, but those wins included
many Bests in Show, Specialty Bests of Breed, Group wins, and
highly prized "Bowl" wins. The Airedale Bowl is offered by the
Airedale Terrier Club of America for Best of Breed at their club

specialties each year. It has been in competition since 1910 as a perpetual trophy, and the names of all past club Best of Breed winners are engraved on it. This is the ultimate win to the true Airedale Fancier.

In the mid-60s, another British Airedale Kennel would enhance American bloodlines. Enjoying great success in England, the Jokyl Airedales, under the ownership of George and Olive Johnson, exported some top dogs to America. The Jokyl line combined well with the Bengal dogs, and through these prominent exports, Jokyl figures prominently in the pedigrees of many of the top-quality American Airedales. Imported to America along with the many influential Bengal stud dogs was a bitch, Eng/Am. Ch. Bengal Springtime, a consistent

Many English breeders enhanced the American Airedale's bloodlines. Eng/ Am. Ch. Jokyl Bengal Lionheart was imported to the US in 1963 by co-owners Sarah Coleman Brock and Mr. and Mrs. Charles Mack.

winner in England in the late 1960s. She was bred once in England and from that litter came Eng. Ch. Bengal Flamboyant, one of the breed's top sires there. After whelping that litter, she came to Bob and Betty Hoisington's Eden Kennels in Tennessee. She was then bred to three different dogs, all from Jokyl: champions Superman; his son, Supermaster; and her own grandson, Spic N Span. It's difficult to comprehend the impact that Springtime had on future American Airedales, but simply put, the list of important dogs and kennels tracing back to her reads like a veritable who's who, with over 400 champions carrying lines back to Springtime.

Because of his intelligence and versatility, the Airedale Terrier has steadily grown in popularity throughout the years.

Most knowledgeable dog breeders will tell you that the strength of any kennel is in its bitches. The British influence on American Airedales continued through a number of the breed's top producing dams. Three California Airedale kennels provide adequate proof. In the early 1950s, Reg and Wilma Carter founded their Dandyaire line when they bred their foundation bitch Ch. Burnweel Bessie to Ch. Aireline Star Monarch, himself six generations down off Ditto. Another line, Coppercrest, was founded in the early 1960s when June Dutcher began with her foundation bitch Ch. Scatterfoot Tim Tam, who was a daughter of Aireline Star Monarch. Ch. Sunnydale's Holiday, the foundation bitch for the Sunnydale line of Jack and Mary Sanderson, was sired by Eng/Am. Ch. Jokyl Superior.

One other bitch that must be mentioned is Prelude of Turith. She was not a champion but an extraordinary producer. Dan Kiedrowski, in a 1989 profile of one of her top-winning sons, paid tribute to her. He wrote, "...we would all recognize

Known as the King of Terriers, the Airedale has had great success in the show ring. Ch. Sunnydale Coppercrest Dinah was Best of Breed at the 1983 ATCA Specialty.

her influence as the breed's modern matriarch in America without ever crossing the pond. Having sent over five top-producing sons, her name can be found in nearly three-quarters of the champions finished in the last few years." By Eng/Arg. Ch. Bengal Tarquin came Ch. Turith Country Cousin and Bengal Turith Comet, who sired the dynamic duo, Ch. Bravo True Grit and Ch. Bravo Starbuck. By Eng. Ch. Siccawei Galliard came Ch. Turith Adonis and Ch. Turith Forrester of Junaken. The fifth famous son was by a Galliard son, Eng. Ch. Saredon Military Man, and produced Eng/Am. Ch. Turith Echelon of Saredon. All have ties right back to Springtime.

These four bitches, along with Springtime, were responsible for hundreds of champions in succeeding generations, with many of today's lines tracing back to these notable ladies. It is important to remember the contribution that the queens of Airedales made to the continuation of the King of Terriers.

CHARACTERISTICS of the Airedale Terrier

All puppies are cuddly and cute. The Airedale baby with his floppy ears, curly puppy coat, and big feet has a special charm that is hard to resist. There is nothing more attractive than a litter of little puppies, nestled together sound asleep, one on top of the other. But in addition to being cute, puppies are living, breathing, and very mischievous little creatures, and they are entirely dependent upon their human owner for everything once they leave their mother and littermates. Furthermore, the innocent-appearing and dependent little Airedale puppy quickly becomes a dynamo of energy possessing adolescent hormones that continuously rage and inspire relentless activity.

All puppies are cute, but it is important to make sure that the Airedale puppy you choose will fit in with your lifestyle and personality.

Buying a dog, especially an Airedale puppy, before being absolutely sure that you want to make that commitment can be a serious mistake. The prospective dog owner must clearly understand the amount of time and work involved in the ownership of any dog. Failure to comprehend the extent of commitment that acquiring a dog demands is one of the primary reasons that so many unwanted canines end their lives in an animal shelter.

Before anyone contemplates the purchase of a dog, there are some very important conditions that must be considered. One of the first questions that must be answered is whether or not the person who will ultimately be responsible for the dog's care and well-being actually wants a dog.

The energetic Airedale makes a great playmate and natural babysitter for children. Jake Sinz and his friend "Monty" participate in Airedale Fun Day.

If the prospective dog owner lives alone, all he or she needs to do is be sure that there is a strong desire to make the necessary commitment that dog ownership entails. In the case of family households, it is vital that the person who will be responsible for the pet's care really wants a dog. In the average household, mothers, even

In terms of grooming, the Airedale Terrier is a high-maintenance breed. The amount of time you wish to devote to grooming should be a consideration before selecting a dog. working mothers, are most often given the additional responsibility of caring for the family pets, regardless of the fact that nowadays mothers also are out in the workplace. All too often they are saddled with the additional chores of feeding and trips to the veterinary hospital with what was supposed to be a family project.

Pets are a wonderful method of teaching children responsibility, but it should be remembered that the enthusiasm that inspires children to promise anything in order to have a new puppy may quickly wane. Who will take care of the puppy once the novelty wears off? Does that person want a dog?

Desire to own a dog aside, does the lifestyle of the family actually provide for responsible dog ownership? If the entire family is away from home from early morning to late at night, who will provide for all of a puppy's needs? Basic care such as feeding, exercise, outdoor access, and the like cannot be provided if no one is home. It is important to realize that a puppy needs more than just the basics; he needs love, affection, and attention, too.

Choosing a purebred Airedale will give you a reasonable assurance of what your puppy will grow up to look like.

Another important factor to consider is whether or not the breed of dog is suitable for the person or the family with which it will be living. Some breeds can handle the rough and tumble play of young children, some cannot. The Airedale is a good choice for children of all ages, provided he has been raised with them and that the youngsters are kind, gentle, and considerate of their dog. Children and dogs go together, as long as the child is aware that the dog is a living being, not a teddy bear or a doll. Of course, a rambunctious Airedale adolescent, at times big and clumsy, could unintentionally injure an infant.

Then there is the matter of coat care. The magnificent broken-coat worn by the King of Terriers is the result of many hours of hard work, done by stripping out the wiry long coat, as well as the soft undercoat. Not only is this a time-consuming job for the groomer using his thumb and forefinger and various stripping knives, but it takes many years of practice to learn.

However, the benefits are great—not only will the dog look his best, he will not shed in the house. The alternative to hand-stripping is using electric clippers to shear off the long coat, saving you and your dog many hours on the grooming table. The end result is attractive, too, but the dog will not have the wiry outer coat, and he will shed.

As great as claims are for any breed's intelligence and trainability, remember that the new dog must be taught every household rule that he is to observe. Some dogs catch on more quickly than others, and puppies are just as inclined to forget or disregard lessons as young human children. As tenacious as the terrier can be, so must be the Airedale owner, because it is consistent rule enforcement that makes for the perfect companion.

CASE FOR THE PUREBRED DOG

As previously mentioned, all puppies are cute. Not all puppies grow up to be particularly attractive adults. What is considered beautiful by one person is not necessarily seen as attractive by another. It is almost impossible to determine what a mixed-breed puppy will look like as an adult. Nor will it be possible to determine if the mixed-breed puppy's temperament is suitable for the person or family who wishes to own him. If the puppy grows up to be too big or too active for the owner, what then will happen to him?

Size and temperament can vary to a degree, even within a purebred breed. Still, selective breeding over many generations has produced dogs that give the would-be owner a reasonable assurance of what the purebred puppy will look and act like as an adult. Points of attractiveness completely aside, this predictability is more important than one might think.

A person who wants a dog to go along on those morning jogs or long-distance runs is not going to be particularly happy with a lethargic or short-legged breed. Nor is the fastidious housekeeper, whose picture of the ideal dog is one that lies quietly at the feet of his master by the hour and never sheds, going to be particularly happy with the shaggy dog with a temperament reminiscent of a hurricane.

Purebred puppies will grow up to look like their adult relatives, and by and large, they will behave pretty much like the rest of their family. Any dog, mixed breed or not, has the potential to be a loving companion. However, a purebred dog offers reasonable assurance that he will not only suit the owner's lifestyle but the person's aesthetic demands as well.

WHO SHOULD OWN AN AIREDALE TERRIER?

The Airedale Terrier is a dog suited to many different purposes. In the family, he fulfills the traditional role as a companion to adults as well as children. He enjoys participating in whatever the family is doing and keeps a watchful eye over each member of his family.

A working couple can also make a good home for an Airedale, provided that the dog is not left outside and is included, whenever possible, in the evening and weekend activities. He needs to feel like he is a full-fledged member of the family. Provisions must be made for the puppy when the family is away from home. Rather than leaving a puppy or teenager unattended and loose in the house, it is best that a safe enclosure be made for him outside. A fenced yard works, but if you enjoy gardening, sharing an attractive garden with a puppy that might enjoy doing some gardening of his own is not going to make you happy. The best thing is a fenced dog run, tucked away on the side

The Airedale can serve many purposes within the family, including being a companion. He enjoys participating in all family activities.

Owners of Airedales must be willing to invest time in training their dog in order to give him a productive outlet for his intelligence and energy. of the house or at the end of the garden—the puppy's home away from home.

Aside from being a wonderful companion dog, the Airedale is a most versatile hunter. Of course, he enjoys going after the traditional terrier game of fox, gophers, moles, raccoons, rats, mice, and even snakes, but would you ever have imagined him in the traditional role of a working gundog? In recent years, the Airedale has had his hunting abilities affirmed and has proven to be proficient at flushing and retrieving pheasants and swimming several miles out into rough water to retrieve geese. His hunting abilities have been likened to a cross between a Chesapeake Bay Retriever and an Irish Water Spaniel.

For members of the family who have an interest in traditional obedience work or exploring the agility competitions becoming so popular today, the Airedale is a good candidate for success in both areas.

CHARACTER OF THE AIREDALE TERRIER

The Airedale is a multi-purpose, versatile, all-around dog—hunter, protector, companion par excellence. Active, affectionate, intelligent, and fun-loving, he is a dog for the whole family to enjoy. He's a jack of all trades and master of some, albeit on his own terms at times.

His size, while being the largest of the terrier family, is still within the designation of medium, considering all breeds. He stands 22 to 24 inches at the shoulder and weighs around 40 to 50 pounds. His medium size makes him a perfect house dog. He thrives on being with his special people, whether that includes a long walk, a jog along the beach, a hop in the car to run some errands, or just curling up in a corner of the family room while his family is watching television. As long as he's participating, he is a happy dog.

An intelligent dog, the Airedale is faithful and loyal to his family and a natural guardian. His imposing stature and fearless nature make his very presence a legitimate burglar alarm. The Airedale has been used in police work and has seen active duty with the armed forces in times of war.

Obedience training is fun with this bright, active dog. He can do it all, from the simple heeling pattern to scent discrimination, and he takes the high jump and broad jump in stride. He has also proven most adept at agility competitions. However, with this aptitude and intellect comes the danger of boredom. Too much training and repetition spells trouble for this dog. Owners must remember that all this training must be lots of fun or their Airedale will quickly lose interest. You've never really known the true meaning of the word "stubborn" until you've met a terrier that has decided that this isn't fun anymore and that he's not doing it. Terriers will never be a precision worker like the Doberman Pinscher or the Shetland Sheepdog, but they can excel in the obedience ring if the trainer is up to the challenge of making it fun, different, and entertaining for them both. Trainers working with terriers need an abundant amount of patience and a great sense of humor, as there will seldom be a dull moment.

STANDARD for the Airedale Terrier

Each country has a governing kennel club, and every kennel club has a standard for each breed that describes an ideal dog. The following is the official American Kennel Club standard for the Airedale Terrier.

Head–Should be well balanced with little apparent difference between the length of skull and foreface.

Skull–Should be long and flat, not too broad between the ears and narrowing very slightly to the eyes. Scalp should be free from wrinkles, stop hardly visible and cheeks level and free from fullness.

Ears–Should be V-shaped with carriage rather to the side of the head, not pointing to the eyes, small but not out of proportion to the size of the dog. The topline of the folded ear should be above the level of the skull.

Ch. Goforit Panache, bred and owned by Helen J. Piperis, winning Best of Breed under judge and author Betty-Anne Stenmark.

Foreface–Should be deep, powerful, strong and muscular. Should be well filled up before the eyes.

Eyes–Should be dark, small, not prominent, full of terrier expression, keenness and intelligence. **Lips**–Should be tight.

Nose–Should be black and not too small.

Teeth–Should be strong and white, free from discoloration or defect. Bite either level or vise-like. A slightly overlapping or scissors bite is permissible without preference.

Neck–Should be of moderate length and thickness gradually widening towards the shoulders. Skin tight, not loose.

Shoulders and Chest–Shoulders long and sloping well into the back. Shoulder blades flat. From the front, chest deep but not broad. The depth of the chest should be approximately on a level with the elbows.

Body–Back should be short, strong and level. Ribs well sprung. Loins muscular and of good width. There should be but little space between the last rib and the hip joint.

BEST OF
BREED

SOUTHERN CALIFORNIA
TERRIER ASSOCIATION

April 1998
COOK

Hindquarters—Should be strong and muscular with no droop.

Tail—The root of the tail should be set well up on the back. It should be carried gaily but not curled over the back. It should be of good strength and substance and of fair length.

Legs—Forelegs should be perfectly straight, with plenty of muscle and bone. Elbows should be perpendicular to the body, working free of sides. Thighs should be long and powerful with muscular second thigh, stifles well bent, not turned either in or out, hocks well let down parallel with each other when viewed from behind. Feet should be small, round and compact with a good depth of pad, well cushioned; the toes moderately arched, not turned either in or out.

Coat—Should be hard, dense and wiry, lying straight and close, covering the dog well over the body and legs. Some of the hardest are crinkling or just slightly waved. At the base of the hard very stiff hair should be a shorter growth of softer hair termed the undercoat.

Color—The head and ears should be tan, the ears being of a darker shade than the rest. Dark markings on either side of the skull are permissible. The legs up to the thighs and elbows and the under-part of the body and chest are also tan and the tan frequently runs into the shoulder. The sides and upper parts of the body should be black or dark grizzle. A red mixture is often found in the black and is not to be considered objectionable. A small white blaze on the chest is a characteristic of certain strains of the breed.

Size—Dogs should measure approximately 23 inches in height at the shoulder; bitches, slightly less. Both sexes should be sturdy, well muscled and boned.

Movement—Movement or action is the crucial test of conformation. Movement should be free. As seen from the front the forelegs should swing perpendicular from the body free from the sides, the feet the same distance apart as the elbows. As seen from the rear the hind legs should be parallel with each other, neither too close nor too far apart, but so placed as to give a strong well-balanced stance and movement. The toes should not be turned either in or out.

Faults—Yellow eyes, hound ears, white feet, soft coat, being much over or under the size limit, being undershot or overshot, having poor movement, are faults which should be severely penalized.

SCALE OF POINTS

Head	10
Neck, shoulders and chest	10
Body	10
Hindquarters and tail	10
Legs and feet	10
Coat	10
Color	5
Size	10
Movement	10
General characteristics and expression	15
TOTAL	**100**

Ch. Brisline's House Special, bred and owned by Georgia McRae.

Approved July 14, 1959

SELECTING the Right Airedale Terrier for You

Once the prospective Airedale owner satisfactorily answers all of the questions relating to responsible ownership, he or she will undoubtedly want to rush out and purchase a puppy immediately. Take care— do not act in haste. The purchase of any dog is an important step, because the well-cared-for dog will live with you for many years. In the case of an Airedale Terrier, this could easily be 10 or 12 years. You will obviously want the dog that you live with for that length of time to be one you will enjoy.

It is extremely important that your Airedale is purchased from a breeder who has earned a reputation over the years for consistently producing dogs that are mentally and physically sound. Not only is a sound and stable temperament of paramount importance, but good breeders also are concerned with vigorous health and longevity. Unfortunately, the buyer must indeed be aware that there are always those who are ready and willing to exploit a breed for financial gain, with no thought given to its health or welfare or to the homes in which the dogs will be living.

The only way a breeder can earn a reputation for producing quality animals is through a well-thought-out breeding program in which rigid selectivity is imposed. Selective breeding is aimed at maintaining the virtues of a breed and eliminating genetic weaknesses. This process is time-consuming and costly. Therefore, responsible Airedale breeders protect their investment by providing the utmost in prenatal care for their brood matrons and maximum care and nutrition for the resulting offspring. Once the puppies arrive, the knowledgeable breeder initiates a well-thought-out socialization process.

The governing kennel clubs in the different countries of the world maintain lists of local breed clubs and breeders that can lead a prospective dog buyer to responsible breeders of quality stock. If you are not sure how to contact a respected breeder in your area, we strongly recommend contacting your local kennel club for recommendations.

The buyer should look for cleanliness in both the dogs and the areas in which the dogs are kept. Cleanliness is the first clue that tells you how much the breeder cares about the dogs he or she owns.

It is extremely important that the buyer knows the character and quality of a puppy's parents. Good temperament and good health are inherited, and if the puppy's parents are not sound in these respects, there is not much likelihood that they will produce offspring that are. Never buy an Airedale from anyone who has no knowledge of the puppy's parents or what kind of care a puppy has been given from birth.

HEALTH CONCERNS

There is every possibility that a reputable breeder resides in your area who will not only be able to provide the right Airedale for you, but will also have one if not both parents of the puppy on the premises. This gives you an opportunity to see firsthand what kind of dogs are in the background of the puppy you are considering. Good breeders are always willing to have you see their dogs and to inspect the facility in which the dogs are raised. These breeders will also be able to discuss problems that exist in the breed and how they deal with these problems. Thankfully, the Airedale is basically a hardy and healthy

Finding a quality Airedale Terrier begins with finding a reputable breeder.

breed. Responsible breeders have been doing a good job of breeding quality Airedales, both sound in mind and in body.

Von Willebrand's Disease

This disease is hereditary in man, swine, and dogs. It is an abnormal condition of the blood-clotting system, not unlike the disease of hemophilia that we know to occur in humans. Von Willebrand's is not a sex-linked disease, whereas hemophilia A is, transmitted by females but occurring only in males. Considerable variation exists in the severity of the disease, meaning some affected dogs will lead a fairly normal life and others will die prematurely because of it. The normal clotting time in dogs is two to five minutes, whereas clotting in affected dogs may exceed ten minutes. Obviously, this can lead to extreme complications if the dog requires surgery at some point in his life. In the 1980s, von Willebrand's disease was of some concern to Airedale breeders. While it continues to be today, the occurrence of this condition has been greatly decreased through careful breeding.

A little puppy is a big responsibility, so be sure that you have carefully considered dog ownership before taking an Airedale home.

Hemophilia B (Christmas Disease)

In the 1980s, there was some incidence of hemophilia B in the Airedale breed, which is another kind of persistent bleeding, more rare than hemophilia A. Originally labeled Christmas disease because it was found in a human family whose surname was Christmas, it is now usually called hemophilia B or deficiency of factor IX, a substance in the blood that is necessary for the formation of plasma thromboplastin. It retards the process of clotting but interferes with it at a point different from that affected by hemophilia A.

Responsible breeders will screen all of their Airedales for genetic problems before breeding in order to produce the best puppies possible.

In dogs, as in humans, hemophilia B is caused by a sex-linked recessive gene, but it is a different gene from that causing hemophilia A. Unfortunately, unlike hemophilia A, where cases can be mild, moderate, and severe, hemophilia B only occurs in the severe form, which may be helpful in eliminating the disease from the gene pool. Incidence of this disease has waned in recent years, but it still merits the attention of any responsible breeder.

Hip Dysplasia

This occurs in almost all breeds of dog and affects both purebreds and mongrels. Simply put, hip dysplasia is a failure of the head of the femur to fit snugly into the acetabulum, with resulting degrees of lameness and faulty movement. The inheritance of the defect is polygenic, which means there is no simple answer to the elimination of the problem. Breeders routinely x-ray their breeding stock and breed only from superior animals that have been graded in the categories deemed acceptable for breeding. While it is important that both the sire and dam have been x-rayed and cleared for breeding, it is just as important that their littermates, their grandparents, and so on, have been x-rayed and their history known. Family selection is at least as important as individual selection in the case of polygenetic diseases. Happily, the incidence of hip dysplasia in Airedales has declined considerably in the last 20 years. Asking a breeder about the hip status on the parents of the litter and about the incidence of hip dysplasia in their line would be appropriate. As a pet owner, it is important for you to know that individual dogs that have hips that might not rate above a grade of "fair" can lead a long and normal life.

Hypothyroidism

Otherwise known as low thyroid function, hypothyroidism is a fairly common health problem in all dogs, purebred and crossbred alike, and affects many older dogs. Most dogs are born with normal thyroid function, but many become affected with hypothyroidism as they age. There are two causes of this condition, one being autoimmune thyroid disease. The other, more common cause is idiopathic hypothyroidism.

The good news about the latter type of hypothyroidism is that the disease is easily diagnosed with a blood test, and treatment is easy and inexpensive (simply a small pill taken once or twice daily). Common indicators of hypothyroidism are lethargy, tendency toward obesity, increased sensitivity to heat and cold, bilateral hair loss, and bilateral blackening of skin, particularly on the abdomen and thighs. Hypothyroidism can also adversely affect reproduction.

QUESTIONS AND ANSWERS

Describing the diseases that can affect the Airedale is not meant to suggest that all Airedale lines are afflicted with them. However, the responsible breeder will always be more than happy to discuss his or her experience, if any, with the problems.

All breeds of dog have genetic problems that must be paid attention to, and just because a male and female do not show evidence of these problems does not mean that their pedigrees are free of something that might be entirely incapacitating. Again, rely upon recommendations from your national kennel club or local breed club when looking for a breeder. A responsible dog breeder will expect to be asked questions.

As we have mentioned previously, do not be surprised if a concerned breeder asks many questions about you and the environment in which your Airedale will be raised. Good breeders are just as concerned with the quality of the homes to which their dogs are going as you, the buyer, are concerned with obtaining a sound and healthy dog.

Before you purchase an Airedale puppy, make sure you have educated yourself about all the medical problems that can affect the breed.

Do not think a good Airedale puppy can only come from a large kennel. On the contrary, many of today's best breeders raise dogs in their homes as a hobby. It is important, however, that you not allow yourself to fall into the hands of an irresponsible "backyard breeder." Backyard breeders separate themselves from the hobby breeder because of their total lack of regard for the health of their breeding stock. They do not test their stock for genetic problems, nor are they concerned with how or where their puppies are raised.

We offer one important bit of advice to the prospective Airedale buyer: If the person is attempting to sell you a puppy with no questions asked—go elsewhere!

RECOGNIZING A HEALTHY PUPPY

Most Airedale breeders do not release their puppies until they have been given their first puppy shots. Normally, this is at about seven to nine weeks of age. At this age, they will bond extremely well with their new owners and are entirely weaned. Nursing puppies receive temporary immunization

Play with the puppy you like away from his mother and littermates. You can tell more about his temperament and see how he reacts to you.

from their mother. Once weaned, however, a puppy is highly susceptible to many infectious diseases that can be transmitted via the hands and clothing of people. Therefore, it behooves you to make sure that your puppy is fully inoculated before he leaves his home environment and to know when any additional inoculations should be given. The responsible breeder will send you out the door with lots of written instructions, including the recommended schedule of vaccinations.

Above all, the Airedale puppy you buy should be a happy, bouncy extrovert. The Airedale's protective instinct develops in adulthood. A shy or suspicious puppy is definitely a poor choice, as is a shy, shrinking-violet puppy or one that appears sick and listless. Selecting a puppy of that sort because you feel sorry for him will undoubtedly lead to heartache and difficulty, to say nothing of the veterinary costs that you may incur in getting the puppy well.

If at all possible, take the puppy that you are interested in away from his littermates and into another room or another part of the kennel. The smells will remain the same for the puppy, so he should still feel secure and maintain his outgoing personality, but it will give you an opportunity to inspect the puppy more closely. A healthy little Airedale puppy will be strong and sturdy to the touch—never bony or obese and bloated. The inside of the puppy's ears should be pink and clean. Dark discharge or a bad odor could indicate ear mites, a sure sign of poor maintenance. The healthy Airedale puppy's breath smells "sweet," that unique scent dog breeders lovingly call "puppy breath." The teeth are clean and white, and there should never be any malformation of the mouth or jaw. The puppy's eyes should be clear and bright and have a soft, almost wise look, which is typical of an Airedale baby. Eyes that appear runny and irritated indicate serious problems.

The puppy you pick should be bright-eyed, outgoing, and curious about the world around him.

There should be no sign of discharge from the nose, nor should it be crusted or runny. However, if the puppies have just come in from outside, do not be surprised to see fresh dirt from a digging escape on the nose and muzzle. Both coughing and diarrhea are danger signals, as are any eruptions on the skin. The coat should be lustrous.

The healthy Airedale puppy's front legs should be straight as little posts and be strong and true. Of course, there is always a chubby, clumsy puppy or two in a litter. Do not mistake this for unsoundness, but if ever you have any doubts, discuss them with the breeder.

MALE OR FEMALE

While both the male and the female are capable of becoming excellent companions and are equally easy to train, consider the fact that a male Airedale will be larger, sometimes 10 or 15 pounds heavier than his sister, and he will have all the muscle power to go with the extra weight. Give serious consideration to your own strength and stature.

There are other sex-related differences to consider as well. While the Airedale Terrier is a clean breed and relatively easy to housetrain, the male provides a sexually related problem. The male of any breed of dog has a natural instinct to lift his leg and mark his territory. The amount of effort that is involved in training the male not to do this varies with the individual dog, but what must be remembered is that a male considers everything in the household to be a part of his territory and has an innate urge to establish this fact. Unfortunately, this may include your designer drapery or newly upholstered sofa.

Happy and healthy Airedale puppies are a reflection of their breeder's good care.

Females, on the other hand, have their own set of problems. Females have semiannual heat cycles that

Although there are differences between male and female Airedales, either one would make a good pet. commence at about six months of age. During these heat cycles lasting approximately 21 days, the female must be confined to avoid soiling her surroundings with the bloody discharge that accompanies estrus. There are "britches" that are sold at pet shops to assist in keeping the female in heat from soiling the area in which she lives. She must also be carefully watched to prevent males from gaining access to her or she will become pregnant. Do not expect the marauding male to be deterred by the britches if your female has them on.

Both of these sexually related problems can be avoided by having the pet Airedale sexually altered. Spaying the female and neutering the male can save the pet owner all the headaches of either of the sexually related problems without changing the character of your Airedale. If there is any change at all in the altered Airedale, it is in making the dog an even more amiable companion. Above all, altering your pet precludes the possibility of its adding to the serious pet overpopulation problem that exists worldwide.

SELECTING A SHOW-PROSPECT PUPPY

If you are considering a show career for your puppy, all the foregoing regarding soundness and health still apply. It must be remembered, though, that spaying and castration are not reversible procedures and once done, eliminate the possibility of ever breeding or showing your Airedale in conformation shows. Altered dogs can, however, be shown in obedience and agility trials and many other competitive events.

There are a good number of additional points to be considered for the show dog as well. First, it should be remembered that the most any breeder can offer is an opinion on the show potential of a particular puppy. The most promising eight-week-old Airedale puppy can grow up to be an average adult. A breeder has no control over this. Any predictions that breeders make about a puppy's future are based upon their experience with past litters that have produced winning show dogs. It is obvious that the more successful a breeder has been in producing winning Airedales over the years, the broader his or her base of comparison will be.

A puppy's potential as a show dog is determined by how closely he adheres to the demands of the standard of the breed. While most breeders concur that there is no such thing as a sure thing when it comes to predicting winners, they are also quick to agree that the older a puppy is, the better the chances are of making any predictions. We have found that it is best to grade a litter and evaluate the puppies at eight weeks of age. Many breeders prefer to run on the promising show-prospect puppies, and as long as they are well socialized during this time, it is to your advantage. The older the puppy, the more the breeder will know about his or her ultimate potential.

It makes little difference to the owner of a pet if his or her Airedale is a bit too small or has a low tail set, nor would it make a difference if a male pup had only one testicle. These faults do not interfere with an Airedale becoming a healthy, loving companion. However, these flaws would keep that Airedale from a winning show career.

While it certainly behooves the prospective buyer of a show-prospect puppy to be as familiar

This is a pup with potential! Brisline's Kept In Style, owned by Carolyn Campbell and Mary Johnson, shows that he has what it takes to be a success.

with the standard of the breed as possible, it is even more important for the buyer to put himself into the hands of a successful and respected breeder of winning Airedales. The experienced breeder knows that there are certain age-related shortcomings in a young Airedale that maturity will take care of, and that there are other faults that completely eliminate the puppy from consideration as a show prospect.

An experienced breeder of a long line of winning show dogs will quite possibly make your decision easy and pick the best puppy for you. There are no guarantees in life, and having a breeder select a show puppy for you is no guarantee either, but chances are that their pick will be better than your choice.

Breeders are always looking for the right homes in which to place their show-prospect puppies. They can be particularly helpful when they know you'd like to show one of their dogs. The important thing to remember when choosing your first show prospect is that cuteness may not be consistent with quality. While showmanship and a charismatic personality are critical to a show dog's success in the ring, those qualities are the frosting on the cake, so to speak. They are the characteristics that put the well-made Airedale over the top.

An extroverted or particularly loving puppy in the litter might decide that he belongs to you. If you are simply looking for a pet, that is the puppy for you. However, if you are genuinely interested in showing your Airedale, you must keep your head, and without disregarding good temperament, give serious consideration to what the standard says a show-type Airedale Terrier must be.

The complete standard of the breed is presented in this book, and there are also a number of other books that can assist the newcomer in learning more about the breed.

Puppy or Adult

A young puppy is not your only option when contemplating the purchase of an Airedale. In some cases, an adult dog may be just the answer. It certainly eliminates the trials and tribulations of housebreaking, chewing, and the myriad problems associated with a young puppy.

On occasion, adult Airedales are available from homes or kennels that breed show dogs. The breeders realize that the older dog would be far happier in a family situation where he can watch TV, take hikes, and be a part of a family instead of living out his life in a kennel run.

Adult Airedales can adjust to their new homes with relative ease. Most new owners are amazed at how quickly it happens and how quickly these adults become devoted to their new families. After all, an Airedale lives to have his own person or family, and even those raised in a kennel seem to blossom in the home environment.

An adult Airedale that has been given kind and loving care in his previous home could be the perfect answer for the elderly or for someone who is forced to be away from home during the day. While it would be unreasonable to expect a young puppy not to relieve himself in the house if you are gone for more than just a few hours, it would be surprising to find a housebroken adult Airedale that would willingly even consider relieving himself in the home in which he lives.

A few adult Airedales may have become set in their ways, and while you may not have to contend with the problems of puppyhood, do realize that there is the rare adult that might have developed habits that do not entirely suit you or your lifestyle. Arrange to

Whether you choose an adult or puppy, the Airedale Terrier can make a wonderful and affectionate companion.

bring an adult Airedale into your home on a trial basis. This way neither you nor the dog will be obligated should either decide you are incompatible.

IDENTIFICATION PAPERS

The purchase of any purebred dog entitles you to three very important documents: a health record containing an inoculation list, a copy of the dog's pedigree, and the registration certificate.

Health Record

Most Airedale breeders have initiated the necessary inoculation series for their puppies by the time they are eight weeks of age. These inoculations protect the puppies against distemper, hepatitis, leptospirosis, parainfluenza, and canine parvovirus. Some breeders also choose to inoculate against infectious diseases and Lyme's disease. In most cases, rabies inoculations are not given until a puppy is four months of age or older.

Adult Airedales can provide you with as much love as a puppy can—without all the hard work of housebreaking and training.

There is a set series of inoculations developed to combat these infectious diseases, and it is extremely important that you obtain a record of the shots your puppy has been given and the dates upon which the shots were administered. This way, the veterinarian you choose will be able to continue with the appropriate inoculation series as needed. Vaccination protocols continually change, and your veterinarian is the best source of information on what is currently deemed best for your puppy.

The breeder will have a stool sample from the litter examined for parasites and have the puppies wormed appropriately, if indicated. Be sure to take a fresh stool sample from your puppy with you when you visit your veterinarian for

Socialization with littermates is very important in order to teach your Airedale to get along with other dogs when he matures.

the first time. Refrigerate the sample if there is more than a couple of hours in between collection and your appointment.

Pedigree

The pedigree is your dog's family tree. The breeder must supply you with a copy of this document authenticating your puppy's ancestors back to at least the third generation. All purebred dogs have a pedigree, which does not imply that a dog is of show quality. It is simply is a chronological list of ancestors.

Registration Certificate

The registration certificate is the canine world's birth

Bring your puppy with you wherever you go—the more people your Airedale meets, the better socialized he will become.

certificate. This certificate is issued by a country's governing kennel club. When you transfer the ownership of your Airedale from the breeder's name to your own name, the transaction is entered on this certificate, and once mailed to the kennel club, permanently recorded in their computerized files. Keep all of these documents in a safe place, as you will need them when you visit your veterinarian or if you ever wish to breed or show your Airedale.

DIET SHEET

Your Airedale is a happy, healthy puppy because the breeder has been carefully feeding and caring for him. Every breeder we know has his or her own particular way of doing this. Most breeders give the new owner a written record that details the amount and kind of food a puppy has been receiving. Follow these recommendations to the letter at least for the first month or two after the puppy comes to live with you.

The diet sheet should indicate the number of times a day your puppy has been accustomed to being fed and the kind of vitamin supplementation, if any, he has been receiving. Following the prescribed procedure will reduce the chance of upset stomach and loose stools.

The breeder will have started your Airedale puppy on the road to good nutrition, so stick to this original diet and make any changes gradually.

Usually a breeder's diet sheet projects the increases and changes in food that will be necessary as your puppy grows from week to week. If the sheet does not include this information, ask the breeder for suggestions regarding increases and the eventual changeover to adult food.

In the unlikely event you are not supplied with a diet sheet by the breeder and are unable to get one, your veterinarian will be able to advise you in this respect. There are countless foods now being manufactured expressly to meet the nutritional needs of puppies and growing dogs. A trip down the pet aisle at your supermarket or pet supply store will prove just how many choices you have. Two important tips to remember: Read labels carefully for content and when dealing with established, reliable manufacturers, you are more likely to get what you pay for.

HEALTH GUARANTEE

Any reputable breeder is more than willing to supply a written agreement that the sale of your Airedale is contingent upon the dog passing a veterinarian's examination. Ideally, you will be able to arrange an appointment with your chosen veterinarian right after you have picked up your puppy from the breeder and before you take the puppy home. If this is not possible, you should not delay this procedure any longer than 24 hours from the time you take your puppy home.

Temperament and Socialization

Temperament is both hereditary and learned. Poor treatment and lack of proper socialization can ruin inherited good temperament. An Airedale puppy that has inherited bad temperament is a poor risk as a companion or as a show dog and should certainly never be bred. Therefore, it is critical that you obtain a happy puppy from a breeder who is determined to produce good temperaments and has taken all the necessary steps to provide the early socialization necessary.

Each puppy is an individual and should be treated as one. Spending time with different people and in different situations will allow your Airedale to develop confidence.

Temperaments in the same litter can range from strong-willed and outgoing on the

If you introduce them to each other at an early age, your Airedale Terrier should get along fine with other pets.

high end of the scale to reserved and retiring at the low end. A puppy that is so bold and strong-willed as to be foolhardy and uncontrollable could easily be a difficult adult that needs a very firm hand. In a breed as large and strong as the Airedale, this would hardly be a dog for the owner who is mild and reserved in demeanor or frail in physique. In every human-canine relationship there must be a pack leader and a follower. In order to achieve his full potential, the Airedale must have an owner who remains in charge at all times. The Airedale wants and needs this kind of relationship.

It is important to remember that an Airedale puppy may be as happy as a clam living at home with you and your family, but if the socialization begun by the breeder is not continued, that sunny disposition will not extend outside your front door. From the day the young Airedale arrives at your home you must be committed to accompanying him upon an unending pilgrimage to meet and co-exist with all human beings and animals. Do not worry about the

Airedale's protective instinct. This comes with maturity.
You should never encourage aggressive behavior on the
part of your puppy, and there never should be any reason
for him to fear strangers.

If you are fortunate enough to have children well past
the toddler stage in the household or living nearby, your
socialization task will be assisted considerably. Airedales
raised with children seem to have a distinct advantage in
socialization. Be aware that children must be supervised so
that they understand how the puppy must be treated.

Airedales are apt to "adopt" the household's children and
make raising the children their own special project.
Children and Airedale puppies seem to understand each
other, and in some way known only to the puppies and
children themselves, they give each other the confidence to
face the trying ordeal of growing up.

The children in your own household are not the only
children your puppy should spend time with. It is a case of
the more the merrier! Every child (and adult for that matter)
that enters your household should be asked to pet your
puppy.

Your puppy should go everywhere with you: the post
office, the market, the shopping mall—wherever. Be
prepared to create a stir wherever you go. The public seems
to hold a special admiration for the Airedale, and while they
might not want to approach a mature dog, most people are
quite taken with the Airedale baby and will undoubtedly
want to pet your youngster. There is nothing in the world
better for the puppy!

If your puppy backs off from a stranger, give the person a
treat to offer him. You must insist that your young Airedale
be amenable to the attention of any strangers you approve
of, regardless of sex, age, or race. It is not up to your puppy
to decide whom he will or will not tolerate. You are in
charge. You must call the shots.

If your Airedale has a show career in his future, there are
other things that will have to be taught in addition to just
being handled. All show dogs must learn to have their
mouths opened and inspected by the judge. The judge must
be able to check the teeth. Males must be accustomed to
having their testicles touched, as the dog show judge must

determine that all male dogs are complete, which means that there are two normal-sized testicles in the scrotum. These inspections must begin in puppyhood and be done on a regular basis.

All Airedales must learn to get along with other dogs as well as with humans. If you are fortunate enough to have a puppy preschool or dog training class nearby, attend with as much regularity as you possibly can. A young Airedale that has been exposed regularly to other dogs from puppyhood will learn to adapt and accept other dogs much more readily than one that seldom ever sees strange dogs.

THE ADOLESCENT AIREDALE TERRIER

You can learn a lot about a puppy's temperament by watching him play with his littermates.

You will find it amazing how quickly the tiny youngster you first brought home begins to develop into a full-grown Airedale Terrier.

Some lines shoot up to full size very rapidly, others mature more slowly. At about five months of age, most Airedale puppies become lanky and ungainly, growing in and out of proportion seemingly from one day to the next.

Somewhere between 12 to 16 months of age, your Airedale will have attained his full height. However, body and muscle development continues on until two years of age in some lines and up to three and almost four in others.

With proper training and socialization, your Airedale puppy can mature into a valuable and welcomed member of the family.

Food needs increase during this growth period, and the average Airedale seems as if he can never get enough to eat. There are some, however, that experience a very finicky stage in their eating habits and seem to eat enough only to keep from starving. Think of Airedale puppies as being as individualistic as children and act accordingly.

The amount of food you give your Airedale should be adjusted to how much he will readily consume at each meal. If the entire meal is eaten quickly, add a small amount to the next feeding and continue to do so as the need increases. Use measuring cups when feeding to make sure that you are increasing the amount by one-quarter or one-third cup—it's always best not to guess. This method will ensure that you give your puppy enough food, but you must also pay close attention to the dog's appearance and condition, as you do not want a puppy to become overweight or obese.

At eight weeks of age, an Airedale puppy is eating three meals a day. By the time he is four months old, the puppy can do well on two meals a day. If your puppy does not eat the food offered, he is either not hungry or not well. Your dog will eat when he is hungry. If you suspect the dog is not well, a trip to the veterinarian is in order.

This adolescent period is a particularly important one because it is the time that your Airedale must learn all the household and social rules by which he will live for the rest of his life. Your patience and commitment during this time will not only produce an obedient canine good citizen, but will forge a bond between the two of you that will grow and ripen into a wonderful relationship.

CARING for Your Airedale Terrier

FEEDING AND NUTRITION

Following the diet sheet provided by the breeder from whom you obtained your puppy is the best way to make sure your Airedale is getting the right amount and the correct type of food for his age. Do your best not to change the puppy's diet and you will be far less apt to run into digestive problems and diarrhea. Diarrhea is something that is very serious in young puppies. Puppies with diarrhea can dehydrate very rapidly, causing severe problems and even death.

If it is necessary to change your puppy's diet for any reason, it should never be done abruptly. Begin by adding a tablespoon or two of the new food and reducing the old product by the same amount. Gradually increase the amount of the new food over a week or ten days until the meal consists entirely of the new product. A puppy's digestive system is extremely delicate. Any changes you make in what he eats should be done carefully and slowly.

The amount of food that you give your Airedale puppy should also be adjusted carefully. Give the puppy all he will eat within 10 or 15 minutes of the time you put the food dish down. Take the dish up after that amount of time has elapsed. If the puppy consumes the entire meal, add a small amount to the next meal, balancing what you add with what the puppy will eat.

There is the occasional Airedale puppy that is a true glutton, and he will eat more than he needs to stay healthy. A rule of thumb is that you should be able to feel the ribs and backbone with just a slight layer of fat and muscle over them. The puppy should be firm to the touch and not sloppy with rolls of loose flesh.

By the time your Airedale puppy is 12 months old, you can reduce feedings to once a day. This meal can be given either in the morning or evening, or if you wish, the single meal can be cut in half and fed twice a day. It is really a matter of choice on your part. There are two important things to remember: Feed the main meal at the same time every day and make sure what you feed is nutritionally complete.

For the dog that eats but one meal per day, a morning or nighttime snack of hard dog biscuits made especially for medium-sized dogs can also be given. These biscuits not only become highly anticipated treats to your Airedale but are also genuinely helpful in maintaining healthy gums and teeth.

Balanced Diets

In the US, dog foods must meet standards set by the Subcommittee on Canine Nutrition of the National Research Council in order to qualify as complete and balanced. As proof of compliance, dog food manufacturers list the ingredients of their product on every box, bag, or can. The ingredients are listed by weight in descending order.

Avoid feeding your Airedale products that contain sugar to any high degree. Excessive amounts of these sugars can lead to severe dental problems and unwanted weight gain.

Consult your breeder or your veterinarian about the appropriate diet for your Airedale Terrier puppy.

To achieve optimum health and condition, make sure your Airedale has a constant supply of fresh, clean water and a balanced diet containing the essential nutrients in correct proportions. This can be achieved

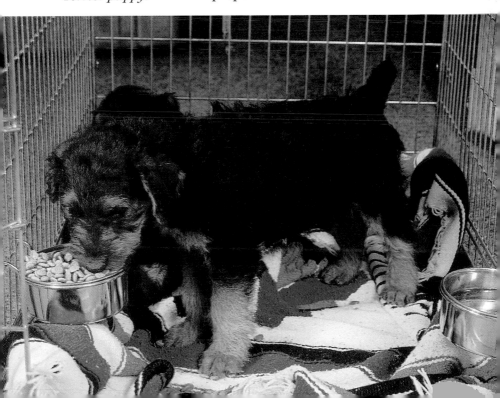

with a good-quality kibble to which a small amount of canned, fresh, or cooked meat can be added. Pet stores and supermarkets all carry a wide selection of foods manufactured by respected companies. An important thing to remember in selecting from these foods is that all dogs are meat-eating animals. Animal protein and fats are important to the well-being of any breed of dog.

The main ingredient in any commercially prepared food you buy should be animal protein. The remaining ingredients in quality products will provide the carbohydrates, fats, roughage, and correct amounts of minerals your dog needs.

Some dry foods may not contain the amount of fat that will keep the Airedale's coat in top condition. If your dog's coat appears dry and seems to lack luster, a very small amount of animal fat, such as bacon drippings or beef trimmings, can be beneficially added to the diet, particularly during winter weather. Some Airedales have a tendency toward "itchy" skin, and sometimes diet can be responsible. One of the dry lamb-and-rice foods might be a simple solution for remedying this problem.

If you give your Airedale treats, make sure they are nutritious and do not upset his regular diet.

Oversupplementation

A great deal of controversy exists today regarding the orthopedic problems that exist in dogs, such as

Proper nutrition is imperative to your dog's health. Veterinarians recommend elevated feeders to help reduce stress on your dog's neck and back muscles. The raised platform also provides better digestion while reducing bloating and gas. Photo courtesy of Pet Zone Products, Ltd.

hip, elbow, and patella (knee) dysplasia. Some experts claim that these problems and a wide variety of chronic skin conditions are entirely hereditary. Others feel they are a result, in whole or in part, of the overuse of mineral and vitamin supplements in puppies and young dogs.

When vitamins are used, the prescribed amount should never be exceeded. Some breeders insist that all recommended dosages be cut in half when used with the heavily fortified commercial foods of the day.

There may be special periods in an Airedale's life when vitamin supplementation is necessary; for example, the rapid growth that the breed experiences in puppyhood, the female's pregnancy, and the time during which she is nursing her puppies. These are high-stress periods, and your veterinarian may suggest vitamin supplementation.

Never feed your Airedale from the table while you are eating. A dog can very quickly become addicted to the exotic smells of the foods you eat and turn up his nose at the less tempting, but probably far more nutritious, food in his regular meals.

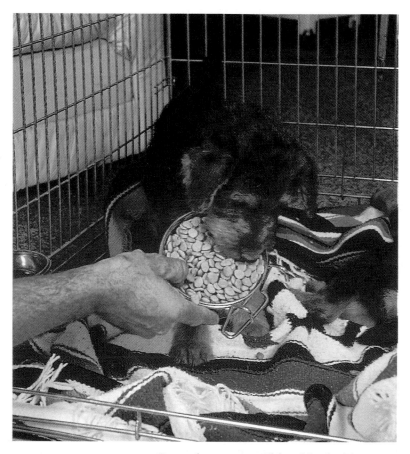

Make sure you choose a good-quality dog food that is appropriate for your Airedale's stage of life and activity level.

Dogs do not care if food looks like a hot dog or wedge of cheese. They only care about the food's smell and taste. Products manufactured to look like other foods are designed to appeal to the humans who buy them. These foods often contain high amounts of preservatives, sugars, and dyes, none of which are suitable for your dog.

Special Diets

There are now countless commercially prepared diets for dogs with special dietary needs. The overweight, underweight, or geriatric dog can have his nutritional needs met, as can puppies and growing dogs. The calorie content of these foods is adjusted accordingly.

Common sense must prevail. What works for humans works for dogs as well—too many calories and too little exercise will increase weight; stepping up exercise and reducing the calorie count will bring weight down.

Occasionally, an adolescent Airedale will become a problem eater. Trying to tempt the dog to eat by handfeeding or offering special foods only serves to make the problem worse.

Bad habits, like begging at the table, can cause your dog to become overweight. Keep your Airedale healthy by staying on a feeding schedule and limiting treats.

Your dog will quickly learn to play the waiting game, fully aware that those special things he likes will arrive—probably sooner than later. Feed your Airedale the proper food you want him to eat. The dog may well turn up his nose a day or two and refuse to eat anything. However, you can rest assured that when your dog is really hungry, he will eat.

Unlike humans, dogs have no suicidal tendencies. A healthy dog will not starve himself to death. He may not eat enough to keep himself in the shape that we find ideal and attractive, but he will definitely eat enough to maintain himself. If your Airedale is not eating properly and appears to be thin and listless, consult your veterinarian.

BATHING AND GROOMING

Bathing

Terrier puppies, with their natural interest in dirt, crawling creatures, and imagined prey, can get pretty dirty in a short time. While a good brushing can remedy a lot of situations, when the puppy is smelly, full of dirt and mud, and you want him in the house with you that evening, a bath is in order. While handlers of show Airedales often avoid bathing the body coat, believing the shampoo softens the wiry coat, there is absolutely no reason why your adult Airedale shouldn't be bathed from time to time. Many older dogs find it invigorating and thoroughly enjoy the attention that a bath and full grooming session brings.

You'll want to have the following items on hand for bathing your dog: a rubber mat for the bottom of the tub, a spray attachment for rinsing, several towels, a "no-tears" shampoo (one of the products for human babies) for around the eyes, and a quality dog shampoo for the rest of the body. If you're concerned about parasites, then make your dog's regular shampoo one of the flea and tick shampoos.

For the puppy's first bath you must have patience, and probably be dressed in your old clothes with a nice big apron tied around you. You can be sure that the moment that the puppy's head is wet, he is going to shake all over. Be kind, patient, and supportive.

Wet the puppy thoroughly with warm water. Do the body and legs first, working the shampoo gently and thoroughly into the coat. The puppy will love this—a full body massage feels great. Use the no-tears shampoo on the head. If you use a flea and tick shampoo, be sure to leave the lather on for the number of minutes recommended or you'll only stun the parasites, not kill them. Rinse the puppy thoroughly until the coat is squeaky clean, and then towel dry him. With the help of a friend to hold and reassure the puppy, you might opt to hurry the drying process by using a blow dryer. Be sure the puppy is thoroughly dry before allowing him to go outside in the cold.

You might consider investing in a grooming table that has a non-slip top and an arm and noose, which can make all of these activities much easier. These tables are available at pet shops or from dog shows. Procedures such as trimming nails, cleaning ears, and checking teeth can be attended to at bath time as well. Undoubtedly, the breeder from whom you purchased your Airedale will have begun to accustom the puppy to grooming just as soon as he was old enough to stand. You must continue with grooming sessions or begin them at once if for some reason they have not been started. It is imperative that you both learn to cooperate in this endeavor in order to make it an easy and pleasant experience.

Nail Trimming

This is a good time to accustom your Airedale to having his nails trimmed and feet inspected. Always look at the bottom of your dog's feet for cracked pads. Check between the toes and pads for splinters, thorns, foxtails, mats, pebbles, etc., paying particular attention to any swollen or tender areas. Use straight scissors to trim the long coat around the feet and between the pads. This will give your dog better traction on slippery floors and stairs.

We suggest that you attend to your dog's nails at least every other week. Long nails on an Airedale are not only unattractive, but they spread and weaken the foot. The nails of an Airedale that isn't exercising outdoors on rough terrain will grow long very quickly. Do not allow them to become overgrown and then expect to cut them back easily. Each nail has a blood vessel running through the center called the quick. The quick grows close to the end of the nail and contains very sensitive nerve endings. If the nail is allowed to grow too long, it will be impossible to cut it back to a proper length without cutting into the quick. This causes the dog severe pain and can

Regular brushing can help keep your Airedale's coat shiny and healthy-looking.

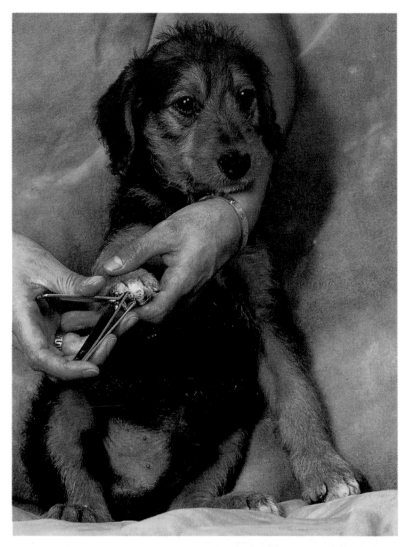

If you accustom your dog to grooming procedures like nail clipping at an early age, he will become used to the process as he matures.

also result in a great deal of bleeding that can be very difficult to stop.

Nails can be trimmed with canine nail clippers or an electric nail grinder (also called a drummel). We prefer to use the fine grinding disc, because it allows you to trim back the nail a little bit at a time, practically eliminating any bleeding from occurring. The Airedale's dark nails make it almost impossible to see where the quick ends, so regardless of which nail trimming device is used, you must proceed with caution and remove only a small portion of the nail at a time.

If the quick is nipped in the trimming process, there are many blood-clotting products available at pet shops that will almost immediately stem the flow of blood. It is wise to have one of these products on hand in case your dog breaks a nail in some way.

Brushing and Combing

Purchase a slicker brush with bent wires mounted in a rubber backing (one of the gentle slickers as opposed to the very rough harsh ones), as well as a steel comb with a combination of medium and coarse teeth.

Pia Lundberg of Sweden has a lot of work ahead of her. Airedales have a double coat that needs lots of care to look its best.

Start at the neck and brush in the direction that the coat grows. Be firm but gentle. Do the entire body and then each leg, being sure to brush in the pits of the forelegs, as this is an area where mats occur. The brushing will remove lots of dead coat. After brushing, go through all the same areas with the coarse section of the comb and then the medium section, and be sure to get right to the skin. Now brush the head and the muzzle, brushing the face coat in the direction it grows, remembering that the dog is always more sensitive around the face than he is the rest of the body. This whole process of brushing and combing won't take but five minutes as long as you remember to do it at least twice, preferably three times each week.

Regular brushing practically eliminates the need to give your Airedale a wet bath. If your dog finds his way into some foul-smelling substance of some kind, there are many dry-bath products that can be used that both clean the coat and eliminate odor.

Hand Stripping

If you have hopes of a career in the conformation show ring for your puppy, then hand stripping the coat is your only option. This is the method of using thumb and forefinger to pluck or pull the dead longer coat out. No, this does not hurt your dog—their coat was designed with this in mind. Sometimes the thumb and forefinger are supplemented by the use of a dull stripping knife to pull, but not cut, the long coat. This is an art form and not something you can learn overnight.

Be sure to clean your Airedale's ears gently and thoroughly, taking special care not to injure him.

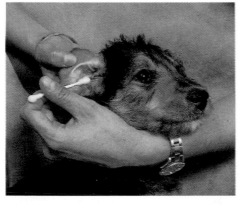

Many of the great groomers will tell you that while their mother liked to embroider or knit as a form of relaxation, they prefer to pull hair on their dogs, finding the act provides a quiet and special time to spend with their dogs.

You can learn a lot about it by reading books and watching videotapes. You will also need the help of your breeder or a knowledgeable friend who can help you get started and critique your work as you go along and learn. Most of the coat work is done at home, before the dog and handler get to the show. Some of the top-winning Airedales will have their coats worked on almost every day of the week. It's no accident that they look spectacular; hours and hours of work have gone into their conditioning. This is most definitely not a wash-and-wear breed!

Clipping

For the Airedale kept as a companion and pet that will never see the conformation show ring, clipping the coat is a viable alternative. Electric clippers with a No. 10 blade are commonly used, clipping in the same pattern that is used when hand stripping. Thinning shears are used to shorten and "post" the

Airedale Terriers that compete in conformation shows must get used to extensive grooming.

legs, as well as trim around the face, beard, chest, and belly, and straight scissors are used for the feet.

Airedales kept as pets can be hand stripped, too, and many pet owners enjoy the effect of the hand stripped body, but will use clippers on the more difficult sections such as the throat and thinning shears for the furnishings and face.

Professional Groomers

Check with your breeder or look in the telephone book for advertisements of groomers that specialize in terriers. A few will offer their services for hand stripping, but this will be costly as it takes hours and hours to accomplish. Some groomers who use clippers can turn out a pretty attractive Airedale trim, but be sure the groomer knows exactly what that means. You don't want to bring home your Airedale wearing a Poodle or Schnauzer haircut!

Teeth Care

Care should always be given to the state of your dog's teeth. If your dog has been accustomed to chewing hard dog biscuits or gnawing on any of the wide variety of Nylabone® products since puppyhood, it is unlikely that he will have any dental problems. For coated breeds, be forewarned that rawhide products and pig's feet often leave a gooey mess on the furnishings on the legs and the feet, and this "treat" may be something you wish to avoid giving your Airedale.

Chewing activity assists greatly in removing dental plaque, which is the major cause of tooth decay. Any sign of redness of the gums or tooth decay merits expert attention. Your veterinarian may recommend daily tooth care using canine toothpaste.

EXERCISE

The Airedale that is given plenty of opportunity to exercise is a much happier and healthier dog. Any dog that expends his energy in physical activity is far less apt to become mischievous and destructive in the home.

Needless to say, puppies should never be forced to exercise. Normally, they are little dynamos of energy and keep themselves busy all day long, interspersing playtime with frequent naps.

As far as the adult Airedale is concerned, he can do pretty much all of the things his owner can do along the lines of exercise: walking, jogging, hiking, swimming, and playing all kinds of games. These activities can do nothing but benefit the Airedale, to say nothing of the dog's owner.

Mature Airedales are capable and enthusiastic jogging companions. They can also be exercised using the Springer bicycle attachment on a bike. It is important, however, to use good judgment with any exercise program. Begin slowly and very gradually increase the distance covered over an extended period of time. Use special precautions in hot weather. High temperatures and forced exercise are a dangerous combination.

SOCIALIZATION

A young Airedale that has never been exposed to strangers, traffic noises, or boisterous children could become confused and frightened. It is important that an Airedale owner give his or her dog the opportunity to experience all of these situations gradually and with his trusted owner present for support.

Airedale puppies are usually friendly and more than happy to accept strangers, but as they mature, their attitudes can change. They can become reserved and suspicious if the socialization process is neglected. It is absolutely imperative that you continue the socialization process and maintain the pack leader role with your Airedale as he matures.

Regular exercise is very important for your Airedale's physical and mental well-being. Arthur Airedale and his friend Edward have fun at the beach.

HOUSEBREAKING and Training Your Airedale Terrier

There is no breed of dog that cannot be trained. Granted, there are some dogs that provide owner's with a real challenge, but in most cases, this has more to do with the trainer and his or her training methods than with the dog's inability to learn. Using the proper approach, any dog that is not mentally deficient can be taught to be a good canine citizen. Many dog owners do not understand how a dog learns, nor do they realize they can be breed specific in their approach to training.

An Airedale Terrier is as smart as his owner allows him to be. The Airedale owner is extremely fortunate in that the breed is not only highly capable of learning, but it also thrives on training.

Even young Airedale puppies have an amazing capacity to learn. This capacity is greater than most humans realize. It is important to remember, though, that these young puppies also forget quickly unless they are reminded of what they have learned by continual reinforcement.

As puppies leave the nest, they began their search for two things: a pack leader and the rules set down by that leader by which the puppies can abide. Dog owners often fail miserably in supplying these very basic needs. Instead, the owner immediately begins to respond to the demands of the puppy, and puppies can quickly learn to be very demanding. In the case of little dogs, this can be a nuisance. In the case of larger dogs like Airedales, this can be obnoxious.

A puppy quickly learns that he will be allowed into the house because he is whining, not because he can only enter the house when he is not whining. Instead of learning that the only way he will be fed is to follow a set procedure (i.e., sitting or lying down on command), the poorly educated Airedale puppy learns that leaping about the kitchen and creating a stir is what gets results.

If your Airedale finds that a growl or a snap can permit him to have his own way, rest assured that this behavior will continue. In fact, the behavior will only increase. On the other hand, if the dog's challenge is met with stern, uncompromising correction, the dog knows that this behavior does not evoke the desired response.

If the young puppy cannot find his pack leader in an owner, the puppy assumes the role of pack leader. If there are no rules imposed, the puppy learns to make his own rules. Unfortunately, the negligent owner continually reinforces the puppy's decisions by allowing the dog to govern the household.

The key to successful training lies in establishing the proper relationship between dog and owner. The owner or the owning family must be the pack leader, and the individual or family must provide the rules by which the dog abides.

Every puppy can benefit from basic training. Eleven-week-old Dion will need time and discipline to become a well-behaved pet.

The Airedale is easily trained to almost any task. It is important to remember, however, that the breed does not comprehend harsh treatment. Positive reinforcement is the key to successfully training an Airedale Terrier, and it produces a happy, confident companion.

An Airedale puppy should always be a winner. Begin teaching simple lessons like the come command when the puppy is already on his way to you. Do not expect the young puppy to come dashing over to you when he is engrossed in some wonderful adventure. The puppy quickly learns that he will be praised for coming on command rather than associating the word with anger on the part of his owner because he did not respond to the word come.

HOUSETRAINING MADE EASY

The method of housetraining we recommend is to prevent accidents from happening. Our motto is, "Puppies don't make mistakes, people do." The young puppy has no idea what housebreaking means; therefore he can hardly be accused of breaking a rule! You must teach the puppy what a fine little tyke he is by attending to his needs outdoors.

We take a puppy outdoors to relieve himself after every meal, after every nap, and after every 15 or 20 minutes of playtime. We carry the puppy outdoors to avoid an accident occurring on the way.

Housetraining is a much easier task with the use of a crate. Most breeders use the fiberglass-type crates approved by the airlines for shipping live animals. They are easy to clean and can be used for the entire life of the dog.

Some first-time dog owners may see the crate method of housebreaking as cruel. What they do not understand is that all dogs need a place of their own to retreat to. A puppy will soon look at his crate as his own private den.

Make sure your Airedale puppy has plenty of time outside to attend to his needs.

Use of a crate reduces housetraining time down to an absolute minimum and avoids keeping a puppy under constant stress by incessantly correcting him for making mistakes in the house. The anti-crate advocates who consider it cruel to confine a puppy for any length of time do not seem to have a problem with constantly harassing and punishing the puppy because he has wet on the carpet and relieved himself behind the sofa.

Begin by feeding your Airedale puppy in the crate. Keep the door closed and latched while the puppy is eating. When the meal is finished, open the cage and carry the puppy outdoors to the spot where you want him to learn to eliminate. In the event that you do not have outdoor access or will be away from home for long periods of time, begin housebreaking by placing newspapers in some out of the way corner that is easily accessible for the puppy. If you consistently take your puppy to the same spot, you will reinforce the habit of going there for that purpose.

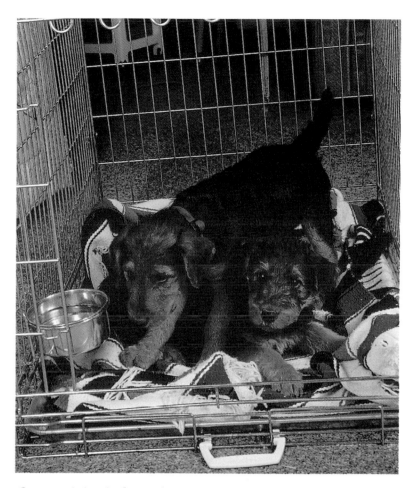

Crate training is the easiest way to housebreak your Airedale, because dogs do not like to soil where they eat and sleep.

It is important that you do not let the puppy loose after eating. Young puppies will eliminate almost immediately after eating or drinking. They will also be ready to relieve themselves when they first wake up and after playing. If you keep a watchful eye on your puppy, you will quickly learn when this is about to take place. A puppy usually circles and sniffs the floor just before he will relieve himself.

Do not give your puppy an opportunity to learn that he can eliminate in the house. If an accident occurs, you must correct the puppy when he is in the act of relieving himself. A puppy does not understand what you are talking about when you reprimand him for something he did even minutes before. Reprimand him at the time of the act or not at all. Your housetraining chores will be reduced considerably if you avoid bad habits in the first place.

If you are not able to watch your puppy every minute, he should be in his cage or crate with the door securely latched. Each time you put your puppy in the crate, give him a small treat of some kind. Throw the treat to the back of the cage and encourage the puppy to walk in on his own. When he does so, praise the puppy and perhaps hand him another piece of the treat through the wires of the cage.

Your Airedale Terrier will soon come to think of his crate as a cozy den in which to retreat and relax.

Do understand that an Airedale puppy of 8 to 12 weeks of age will not be able to contain himself for long periods of time. Puppies of that age must relieve themselves often, except at night. Never leave a very young puppy in a crate for more than four hours during the day. Your schedule must be adjusted accordingly. Also, make sure your puppy has relieved himself at night before the last member of the family retires.

Your first priority in the morning is to get the puppy outdoors. Just how early this will take place will depend much more on your puppy than on you. If your Airedale puppy is like most others, there will be no doubt in your mind when he needs to be let out. You will also very quickly learn to tell the difference between the puppy's "emergency" signals and just unhappy grumbling. Do not test the young puppy's ability to contain himself. His vocal demand to be let out is confirmation that the housebreaking lesson is being learned.

If you find it necessary to be away from home all day, you will not be able to leave your puppy in a crate. On the other hand, do not make the mistake of allowing him to roam the house or even a large room at will. Confine the puppy to a small room or partitioned-off area and cover the floor with newspaper. Make this area large enough so that the puppy will not have to relieve himself next to his bed, food, or water bowls. You will soon find that the puppy will be inclined to use one particular spot to perform his bowel and bladder

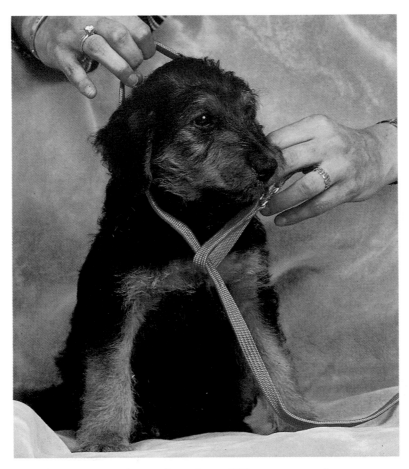

Your puppy must get used to wearing a collar and leash, not only for his safety but for the safety of others.

functions. When you are home, you must take the puppy to this exact spot to eliminate at the appropriate time.

BASIC TRAINING

The Airedale is a ready, willing, and eager student. As previously stated, the breed thrives on learning. Make sure you are also in the right frame of mind for training sessions. Training should never take place when you are irritated, distressed, or preoccupied. Nor should you begin basic training in crowded or noisy places that will interfere with you or your dog's concentration. Once the commands are understood and learned, you can begin testing your dog in public places, but at first the two of you should work in a place where you can concentrate fully upon each other.

The No Command

For his own safety, the most important command your Airedale puppy will ever learn is the meaning of the word no. This is the command the puppy can begin learning the minute he first arrives in your home. It is not necessary to frighten the puppy into learning the meaning of the no command, but it is critical that you never give this or any other command you are not prepared and able to enforce. The only way a puppy learns to obey commands is to realize that once issued, commands must be complied with.

Your Airedale must learn the household rules by which he must abide. Obviously, "Rosie" is allowed to get comfortable with her friend Claire Collins.

Leash or Lead Training

It is never too early to accustom your Airedale puppy to his leash and collar. The leash and collar are your fail-safe way of keeping your dog under control. It may not be necessary for the puppy or adult Airedale to wear his collar and identification tags within the confines of your home, but no dog should ever leave home without a collar and without the leash held securely in your hand. In some countries it is against the law to take your dog out in public places without a collar and lead.

It is best to begin getting your puppy accustomed to this by leaving a soft collar around his neck for a few minutes at a time. Gradually extend the time you leave the collar on. Most Airedale puppies become accustomed to their collar very quickly, and after a few scratches to remove it, forget they are even wearing one.

While you are playing with the puppy, attach a lightweight leash to the collar. Do not try to guide him at first. The point is to accustom the puppy to the feeling of having something attached to the collar.

Encourage your puppy to follow you as you move away. If he is reluctant to cooperate, coax him along with a treat of some kind. Hold the treat in front of the puppy's nose to encourage him to follow you. Just as soon as the puppy takes a few steps toward you, praise him enthusiastically and continue to do so as you move along.

Make the initial sessions short and fun. Continue the lessons in your home or yard until the puppy is completely unconcerned about the fact that he is on a leash. With a treat in one hand and the leash in the other, you can begin to use both to guide the puppy in the direction you wish to go. Begin your first walks in front of the house and eventually extend them down the street and around the block.

The Come Command

The next most important lesson for the Airedale puppy to learn is to come when called. Therefore, it is very important that he learn his name as soon as possible. Constantly repeating the dog's name is what does the trick—use the puppy's name every time you speak to him. "Want to go outside, Rex? Come Rex, come!"

Learning to come on command could save your Airedale's life when the two of you venture out into the world. Come is the command that a dog must understand must be obeyed without question, but the dog should not associate that command with fear. Your dog's response to his name and the word "come" should always be associated with a pleasant experience, such as great praise and petting or a food treat. All too often, novice trainers get very angry at their dog for not responding immediately to the come command. When the dog finally does come after a chase, the owner scolds the dog for not obeying. The dog begins to associate the come command with an unpleasant result.

It is much easier to avoid the establishment of bad habits than it is to correct them once set. At all costs, avoid giving the come command unless you are sure your puppy will come to you.

The very young puppy is far more inclined to respond to learning the come command than the older dog. Use the command initially when the puppy is already on his way to you or give the command while walking or running away from the youngster. Clap your hands and sound very happy and excited about having the puppy join in on this "game."

The very young Airedale will normally want to stay as close to his owner as possible, especially in strange surroundings. When your puppy sees you moving away, his natural inclination will be to get close to you. This is a perfect time to use the come command.

Later, as a puppy grows more self-confident and independent, you may want to attach a long leash or rope to the puppy's collar to ensure the correct response. Again, do not chase or punish your puppy for not obeying the come command. Doing so in the initial stages of training makes the youngster associate the command with something to fear, and this will result in avoidance rather than the immediate positive response you desire. It is imperative that you praise your puppy

Treats and toys can be great training motivators for your Airedale puppy.

and give him a treat when he does come to you, even if he voluntarily delays responding for many minutes.

The Sit and Stay Commands

Just as important to your Airedale's safety (and your sanity!) as the no command and learning to come when called are the sit and stay commands. Many Airedale puppies learn the sit command easily, often in just a few minutes, especially if it appears to be a game and a food treat is involved.

Your puppy should always be on a collar and leash for his lessons. Young puppies are not beyond getting up and walking away when they have decided you and your lessons are boring.

Your Airedale will want nothing more than to please you. Praise and affection are an important part of the training process.

Give the sit command immediately before gently pushing down on your puppy's hindquarters or scooping his hind legs from under him, molding him into a sit position. Praise the puppy lavishly when he does sit, even though it was you who made the action take place. Again, a food treat always seems to get the lesson across to the learning youngster.

Continue to lightly hold the dog's rear end down and repeat the sit command several times. If your dog makes an attempt to get up, repeat the command yet again while exerting light pressure on the rear end until the correct position is assumed. Make your Airedale stay in this position for increasing lengths of time. Begin with a few seconds and increase the time as lessons progress over the following weeks.

If your young student attempts to get up or to lie down, he should be corrected by simply saying, "Sit!" in a firm voice. This should be accompanied by returning the dog to the desired position. Only when you decide your dog should get up should he be allowed to do so.

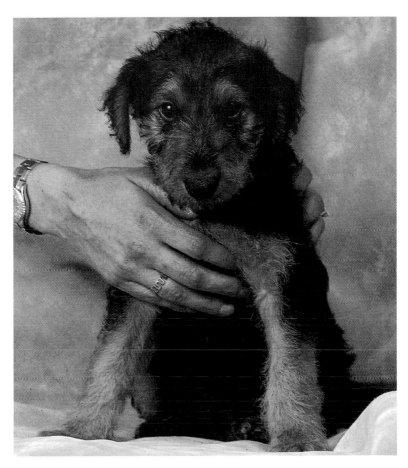

The sit is the foundation for all other commands, because it helps teach your puppy self-control.

Do not test the limits of a very young puppy's patience. As brilliant as the Airedale Terrier is, remember that you are dealing with a baby. The attention span of any youngster, canine or human, is relatively short.

When you do decide your puppy can get up, call his name, say, "OK," and make a big fuss over him. Praise and a food treat are in order every time your puppy responds correctly. Continue to help your puppy assume proper positions or respond to commands until he performs on his own. This way, the puppy always wins—he gets it right every time. You are training with positive reinforcement.

Once your puppy has mastered the sit lesson, you may start on the stay command. With your dog on leash and facing you, command him to "Sit," then take a step or two back. If your dog attempts to get up to follow, firmly say, "Sit, stay!" While you are saying this raise your hand, palm toward the dog, and again command, "Stay!"

Any attempt on your dog's part to get up must be corrected at once, returning him to the sit position and repeating, "Stay!" Once your Airedale begins to understand what you want, you can gradually increase the distance you step back. With a long leash attached to your dog's collar (even a clothesline will do), start with a few steps and gradually increase the distance to several yards. Your Airedale must eventually learn that the sit/stay command must be obeyed no matter how far away you are. Later on, with advanced training, your dog will learn that the command is to be obeyed even when you move entirely out of sight.

Because it represents submission, the down command may be difficult for your Airedale to master. Teller, owned by Carole Bullwinkle Foucrault, seems to have no problem.

As your Airedale masters this lesson and is able to remain in the sit position for as long as you dictate, avoid calling your dog to you at first. This makes the dog

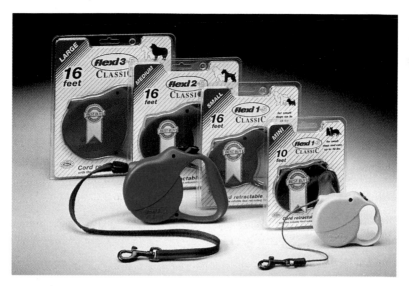

Retractable leashes provide dogs freedom while allowing the owner to keep command at all times. Leashes are available in a wide variety of lengths for all breeds of dogs. Photo courtesy of Flexi-USA, Inc.

overly anxious to get up and run to you. Instead, walk back to your dog and say, "OK," which is a signal that the command is over. Later, when your Airedale becomes more reliable in this respect, you can call him to you.

It is best to keep the "stay" part of the lesson to a minimum until the puppy is at least five or six months old. Everything in a very young Airedale's makeup urges him to stay close to you wherever you go. The puppy has bonded to you and forcing him to operate against his natural instincts can be bewildering to him.

The Down Command

Once your Airedale has mastered the sit and stay commands, you may begin work on the down command. This is the single word command for lie down. Use the down command only when you want the dog to lie down. If you want your dog to get off your sofa or to stop jumping up on people, use the "off" command. Do not interchange these two commands. Doing so will only serve to confuse your dog, after which evoking the right response will become next to impossible.

The down position is especially useful if you want your Airedale to remain in a particular place for a long period of time. A dog is usually far more inclined to stay put when he is lying down than when he is sitting.

Teaching this command to your Airedale may take a little more time and patience than the previous lessons. It is believed by some animal behaviorists that assuming the down position somehow represents submissiveness to the dog.

With your Airedale sitting in front of and facing you, hold a treat in your right hand and the excess part of the leash in your left hand. Hold the treat under the dog's nose and slowly bring your hand down to the ground. Your dog will follow the treat with his head and neck. As he does, give the command, "Down," and exert light pressure on the dog's shoulders with your left hand. If your dog resists the pressure on his shoulders, do not continue pushing down. Doing so will only create more resistance.

When learning to heel, your Airedale should walk on your left side with his shoulder next to your leg, no matter which direction you go.

An alternative method you can use to get your Airedale headed into the down position is to move around to the dog's right side and as you draw his attention downward with your right hand, slide your left arm under the dog's front legs and gently slide them forward. In the case of a small puppy, you will undoubtedly have to be on your knees next to the youngster.

As your Airedale's forelegs begin to slide out to his front, keep moving the treat along the ground until the dog's whole body is lying on the ground, while you continually repeat, "Down." Once your Airedale has assumed the position you desire, give him the treat and a lot of praise. Continue assisting your dog into the down position until he does so on his own. Be firm and be patient.

The Heel Command

In learning to heel, your Airedale will walk on your left side with his shoulder next to your leg, no matter which direction you might go or how quickly you turn. It is also very important for your dog to understand this command when the two of you are out walking. Teaching your Airedale to heel will not only

make your daily walks far more enjoyable, it will make him a far more tractable companion when the two of you are in crowded or confusing situations. Understand that some uninformed people are frightened when they see an Airedale coming down the street. An Airedale lunging at the end of the leash, even if it is done to greet the passerby, can be extremely intimidating.

We have found that a lightweight, link-chain training collar is very useful for the heeling lesson. It provides both quick pressure around the neck and a snapping sound, both of which get the dog's attention. Erroneously referred to as a "choke collar," the link-chain collar, when used properly, does not choke the dog. The pet shop at which you purchase the training collar will be able to show you the proper way to put it on your dog. Do not leave this collar on your puppy when training sessions are finished. Because the collars fit loosely, they can get hooked and cause injury or even death.

As you train your puppy to walk along on the leash, you should accustom the youngster to walking on your left side. The leash should cross your body from the dog's collar to your right hand. The excess portion of the leash will be folded into your right hand and your left hand will be used to make corrections with the leash.

A quick short jerk on the leash with your left hand will keep your dog from lunging side to side, pulling ahead, or lagging back. As you make a correction, give the heel command. Keep the leash slack as long as your dog maintains the proper position at your side.

If your dog begins to drift away, give the leash a sharp jerk, guide the dog back to the correct position, and give the heel command. Do not pull on the lead with steady pressure. What is needed is a sharp but gentle jerking motion to get your dog's attention.

Training Classes

As we mentioned before, the Airedale is only limited in his education by you. There are few limits to what a patient, consistent owner can teach his or her Airedale. For advanced obedience work beyond the basics, it is wise for the Airedale owner to consider local professional assistance. Professional trainers have had long-standing experience in avoiding the pitfalls of obedience training and can help you to avoid these mistakes as well. Airedale owners who have never trained a dog before have found, with professional assistance, that their dog has become a superstar in obedience circles.

This training assistance can be obtained in many ways. Classes are particularly good for your Airedale's socialization. The dog will learn that he must obey even when there are other dogs and people around. These classes also keep the Airedale ever mindful of the fact that he must get along with other people and other dogs. There are free-of-charge classes at many parks and recreation facilities, as well as very formal and sometimes very expensive individual lessons with private trainers.

There are also some obedience schools that will take your Airedale and train him for you. An Airedale can and will learn with any good professional as long as the trainer is gentle. However, unless your schedule provides no time at all to train your own dog, having someone else train the dog for you would be last on our list of recommendations. The rapport

Training class is a great place for your Airedale to learn basic obedience, as well as a good way for him to socialize with other dogs.

that develops between the owner who has trained his or her Airedale to be a pleasant companion and good canine citizen is very special—well worth the time and patience it requires to achieve.

Versatility

The versatility of the Airedale Terrier as a hunting companion cannot be over emphasized. Over a 100 years ago, Mr. Reginald Knight extolled their virtues in Vero Shaw's book, *The Classic Encyclopedia of the Dog*: "They were used by working men for water-side hunting after rats, water-hens, ducks, and in fact, anything that might turn up. They are also used for poaching hares and rabbits, the gates in the field being quietly netted, and the dog then sent in to 'seek up.' He would hunt the entire field over without ever a whimper, if properly trained to it. If broken to the gun they are one of the best sporting dogs out, as they will hunt, retrieve, and set and carry either 'fur or feather' without hardly a mark, and yet, if told, will chase and kill and almost catch anything. I need not tell you how game they are, as many of them have been known to stand up for an hour and forty minutes to Bull-terriers."

The possibilities of sharing enjoyable experiences with your Airedale are endless. Airedales seem to excel in just about anything a dog is capable of doing—hunting, police work, obedience and agility trials, and sentry duty and messenger work in times of war. Many Airedales are used as therapy dogs for the aged or infirm. It is amazing how gentle even the most robust young male can be with fragile people.

Fun and Games

There are many opportunities for you to spend quality time with your Airedale that will provide exercise for both of you and valuable training for your dog. The American Kennel Club offers conformation and obedience classes, agility events, and tracking tests. There are also activities like scent hurdle racing, flyball, and Frisbee.

With an Airedale Terrier, the possibilities are endless. With hard work and training, there is nothing you can't do together.

Owning an Airedale is like having a best friend. This friend, however, loves doing anything and everything you enjoy, when and where you want to do it. Can you ask for more?

SPORT of Purebred Dogs

Welcome to the exciting and sometimes frustrating sport of dogs. No doubt you are trying to learn more about dogs or you wouldn't be deep into this book. This section covers the basics that may entice you, further your knowledge, and help you to understand the dog world.

Dog showing has been a very popular sport for a long time and has been taken quite seriously by some. Others only enjoy it as a hobby.

The Kennel Club in England was formed in 1859, the American Kennel Club was established in 1884, and the Canadian Kennel Club was formed in 1888. The purpose of these clubs was to register purebred dogs and maintain their Stud Books. In the

Successful showing requires dedication and preparation. Ch. Finlair Tiger of Stone Ridge, with handler Bob LaRouech, at his last appearance at the Montgomery Kennel Club.

beginning, the concept of registering dogs was not readily accepted. More than 36 million dogs have been enrolled in the AKC Stud Book since its inception in 1888. Presently the kennel clubs not only register dogs but adopt and enforce rules and regulations governing dog shows, obedience trials, and field trials. Over the years they have fostered and encouraged interest in the health and welfare of the purebred dog. They routinely donate funds to veterinary research for study on genetic disorders.

Below are the addresses of the kennel clubs in the United States, Great Britain, and Canada.

The American Kennel Club
260 Madison Avenue
New York, NY 10016
(Their registry is located at: 5580 Centerview Drive, STE 200, Raleigh, NC 27606-3390)

Ch. Brisline's Nice Catch, bred by Georgia McRae, completing her championship at the Montgomery County Kennel Club in 1998.

The Kennel Club
1 Clarges Street
Piccadilly, London, WIY 8AB, England

The Canadian Kennel Club
100-89 Skyway Avenue
Etobicoke, Ontario M6S 4V7
Canada

Today there are numerous activities that are enjoyable for both the dog and the handler. Some of the activities include conformation showing, obedience competition, tracking, agility, the Canine Good Citizen Certificate, and a wide range of instinct tests that vary from breed to breed. Where you start depends upon your goals which early on may not be readily apparent.

Puppy Kindergarten

Every puppy will benefit from this class. PKT is the foundation for all future dog activities from conformation to "couch potatoes." Pet owners should make an effort to attend even if they never expect to show their dog. The class is designed for puppies about three months of age with graduation at approximately five months of age. All the puppies will be in the same age group and, even though some may be a little unruly, there should not be any real problem. This class will teach the puppy some beginning obedience. As in all obedience classes, the owner learns how to train his own dog. The PKT class gives the puppy the opportunity to interact with other puppies in the same age group and exposes him to strangers, which is very important. Some dogs grow up with behavior problems, one of them being fear of strangers. As you can see, there can be much to gain from this class.

No matter what is in store for your Airedale puppy in the future, he should have the benefit of going to puppy kindergarten.

There are some basic obedience exercises that every dog should learn. Some of these can be started with puppy kindergarten.

Conformation

Conformation showing is our oldest dog show sport. This type of showing is based on the dog's appearance—that is, his structure, movement, and attitude. When considering this type of showing, you need to be aware of your breed's standard and be able to evaluate your dog compared to that standard. The breeder of your puppy or other experienced breeders would be good sources for such an evaluation. Puppies can go through lots of changes over a period of time. Many puppies start out as promising hopefuls and then after maturing may be disappointing as show candidates. Even so, this should not deter them from being excellent pets.

Usually conformation training classes are offered by the local kennel or obedience clubs. These are excellent places for training puppies. The puppy should be able to walk on a lead before entering such a class. Proper ring procedure and technique for posing (stacking) the dog will be demonstrated as well as gaiting the dog. Usually certain patterns are used in the ring such as the triangle or the "L." Conformation class, like the PKT class, will give your youngster the opportunity to socialize with different breeds of dog and humans too.

It takes some time to learn the routine of conformation showing. Usually one starts at the puppy matches that may be AKC Sanctioned or Fun Matches. These matches are generally for puppies from two or three months to a year old, and there may be classes for the adult over the age of 12 months. Similar to point shows, the classes are divided by sex and after completion of the classes in that breed or variety, the class winners compete for Best of Breed or Variety. The winner goes

Ch. Finlair Isis winning Best of Breed at the 1995 Airedale Terrier Club of America National Specialty.

In conformation, your Airedale Terrier will be judged on how closely he conforms to the standard of the breed.

on to compete in the Group and the Group winners compete for Best in Match. No championship points are awarded for match wins.

A few matches can be great training for puppies even though there is no intention to go on showing. Matches enable the puppy to meet new people and be handled by a stranger—the judge. It is also a change of environment, which broadens the horizon for both dog and handler. Matches and other dog activities boost the confidence of the handler and especially the younger handlers.

Earning an AKC championship is built on a point system, which is different from Great Britain. To become an AKC Champion of Record the dog must earn 15 points. The number of points earned each time depends upon the number of dogs in competition. The number of points available at each show depends upon the breed, its sex, and the location of the show. The United States is divided into ten AKC zones. Each zone has its own set of points. The purpose of the zones is to try to equalize the points available from breed to breed and area to area. The AKC adjusts the point scale annually.

The number of points that can be won at a show are between one and five. Three-, four-, and five-point wins are considered majors. Not only does the dog need 15 points won under three different judges, but those points must include two majors under two different judges. Canada also works on a point system but majors are not required.

Dogs always show before bitches. The classes available to those seeking points are: Puppy (which may be divided into 6 to 9 months and 9 to 12 months); 12 to 18 months; Novice; Bred-by-Exhibitor; American-bred; and Open. The class winners of the same sex of each breed or variety compete against each other for Winners Dog and Winners Bitch. A Reserve Winners Dog and Reserve Winners Bitch are also awarded but do not carry any points unless the Winners win is disallowed by AKC. The Winners Dog and Bitch compete with the specials (those dogs that have attained championship) for Best of Breed or Variety, Best of Winners and Best of Opposite Sex. It is possible to pick up an extra point or even a major if the points are higher for the defeated winner than those of Best of Winners. The latter would get the higher total from the defeated winner.

At an all-breed show, each Best of Breed or Variety winner will go on to his respective Group and then the Group winners will compete against each other for Best in Show. There are seven Groups: Sporting, Hounds, Working, Terriers, Toys, Non-Sporting, and Herding. Obviously, there are no Groups at speciality shows (those shows that have only one breed or a show such as the American Spaniel Club's Flushing Spaniel Show, which is for all flushing spaniel breeds).

Earning a championship in England is somewhat different since they do not have a point system. Challenge Certificates are awarded if the judge feels the dog is deserving regardless of the number of dogs in competition. A dog must earn three Challenge Certificates under three different judges, with at least one of these Certificates being won after the age of 12 months. Competition is very strong and entries may be higher than they are in the US. The Kennel Club's Challenge Certificates are only available at Championship Shows.

In England, The Kennel Club regulations require that certain dogs, Border Collies and Gundog breeds, qualify in a working capacity (i.e., obedience or field trials) before becoming a full

Champion. If they do not qualify in the working aspect, then they are designated a Show Champion, which is equivalent to the AKC's Champion of Record. A Gundog may be granted the title of Field Trial Champion (FT Ch.) if he passes all the tests in the field but would also have to qualify in conformation before becoming a full Champion. A Border Collie that earns the title of Obedience Champion (Ob Ch.) must also qualify in the conformation ring before becoming a Champion.

The US doesn't have a designation full Champion but does award for Dual and Triple Champions. The Dual Champion must be a Champion of Record, and either Champion Tracker, Herding Champion, Obedience Trial Champion, or Field Champion. Any dog that has been awarded the titles of Champion of Record, and any two of the following: Champion Tracker, Herding Champion, Obedience Trial Champion, or Field Champion, may be designated as a Triple Champion.

Ch. Terrydale's Adorable Lady, bred and owned by Steve and Mary Clark.

The shows in England seem to put more emphasis on breeder judges than those in the US. There is much competition within the breeds. Therefore the quality of the individual breeds should be very good. In the United States we tend to have more "all around judges" (those that judge multiple breeds) and use the breeder judges at the specialty shows. Breeder judges are more familiar with their own breed since they are actively breeding that breed or did so at one time. Americans emphasize Group and Best in Show wins and promote them accordingly.

The shows in England can be very large and extend over several days, with the Groups being scheduled on different days. Though multi-day shows are not common in the US, there are cluster shows, where several different clubs will use the same show site over consecutive days.

Westminster Kennel Club is our most prestigious show, although the entry is limited to 2500. In recent years, entry has been limited to Champions. This show is more formal than the majority of the shows with the judges wearing formal attire and the handlers fashionably dressed. In most instances the quality of the dogs is superb. After all, it is a show of Champions. It is a good show to study the AKC registered breeds and is by far the most exciting—especially since it is televised! WKC is one of the few shows in this country that is still benched. This means the dog must be in his benched area during the show hours except when he is being groomed, in the ring, or being exercised.

Typically, the handlers are very particular about their appearances. They are careful not to wear something that will detract from their dog but will perhaps enhance it. American ring procedure is quite formal compared to that of other countries. There is a certain etiquette expected between the judge and exhibitor and among the other exhibitors. Of course, it is not always the case but the judge is supposed to be polite, not engaging in small talk or acknowledging how well he knows the handler. There is a more informal and relaxed atmosphere at the shows in other countries. For instance, the dress code is more casual. I can see where this might be more fun for the exhibitor and especially for the novice. The US is very handler-oriented in many of the breeds. It is true, in most instances, that the experienced professional handler can present the dog better and will have a feel for what a judge likes.

In England, Crufts is The Kennel Club's own show and is most assuredly the largest dog show in the world. They've been known to have an entry of nearly 20,000, and the show lasts four days. Entry is only gained by qualifying through winning in specified classes at another Championship Show. Westminster is strictly conformation, but Crufts exhibitors and spectators enjoy not only conformation but obedience, agility, and a multitude of exhibitions as well. Obedience was admitted in 1957 and agility in 1983.

Westminster is one of the most prestigious dog shows in the US. Ch. Serendipity Eagle's Wings, shown by handler Andrew Green to judge Ken McDermott at the 1996 Westminster Kennel Club show.

If you are handling your own dog, please give some consideration to your apparel. For sure, the dress code at matches is more informal than the point shows. However, you should wear something a little more appropriate than beach attire or ragged jeans and bare feet. If you check out the handlers and see what is presently fashionable, you'll catch on. Men usually dress with a shirt and tie and a nice sports coat. Whether you are male or female, you will want to wear comfortable clothes and shoes. You need to be able to run with your dog and you certainly don't want to take a chance of falling and hurting yourself. Heaven forbid, if nothing else, you'll upset your dog. Women usually wear a dress or two-piece outfit, preferably with pockets to carry bait, comb, brush, etc. In this case men are the lucky ones with all their pockets. Ladies, think about where your dress will be if you need to kneel on the floor and also think about running. Does it allow freedom to do so?

Handlers should wear comfortable clothes that do not distract from the appearance of their dog and allow them to move freely about the ring.

You need to take along dog; crate; ex pen (if you use one); extra newspaper; water pail and water; all required grooming equipment, including hair dryer and extension cord; table; chair for you; bait for dog and lunch for you and friends; and, last but not least, clean up materials, such as plastic bags, paper towels, and perhaps a bath towel and some shampoo—just in case. Don't forget your entry confirmation and directions to the show.

If you are showing in obedience, then you will want to wear pants. Many of our top obedience handlers wear pants that are color-coordinated with their dogs. The philosophy is that imperfections in the black dog will be less obvious next to your black pants.

Many Airedales have excelled in the show ring. Ch. Finlair Tiger of Stone Ridge, a top-winning Airedale, has won 25 Bests in Show and 13 Bests of Breed at specialty shows.

Whether you are showing in conformation, Junior Showmanship, or obedience, you need to watch the clock and be sure you are not late. It is customary to pick up your conformation armband a few minutes before the start of the class. They will not wait for you and if you are on the show grounds and not in the ring, you will upset everyone. It's a little more complicated picking up your obedience armband if you show later in the class. If you have not picked up your armband and they get to your number, you may not be allowed to show. It's best to pick up your armband early, but then you may show earlier than expected if other handlers don't pick up. Customarily all conflicts should be discussed with the judge prior to the start of the class.

Junior Showmanship

The Junior Showmanship Class is a wonderful way to build self-confidence even if there are no aspirations of staying with the dog-show game later in life. Frequently, Junior Showmanship becomes the background of those who become successful exhibitors/handlers in the future. In some instances it is taken very seriously, and success is measured in terms of wins. The Junior Handler is judged solely on his ability and skill in presenting his dog. The dog's conformation is not to be considered by the judge. Even so, the condition and grooming of the dog may be a reflection upon the handler.

Usually the matches and point shows include different classes. The Junior Handler's dog may be entered in a breed or obedience class and even shown by another person in that class. Junior Showmanship classes are usually divided by age and perhaps sex. The age is determined by the handler's age on the day of the show. The classes are:

Novice Junior for those at least 10 and under 14 years of age who at the time of entry closing have not won three first places in a Novice Class at a licensed or member show.

Novice Senior for those at least 14 and under 18 years of age who at the time of entry closing have not won three first places in a Novice Class at a licensed or member show.

Open Junior for those at least 10 and under 14 years of age who at the time of entry closing have won at least three first places in a Novice Junior Showmanship Class at a licensed or member show with competition present.

Open Senior for those at least 14 and under 18 years of age who at the time of entry closing have won at least three first places in a Novice Junior Showmanship Class at a licensed or member show with competition present.

Junior Handlers must include their AKC Junior Handler number on each show entry. This needs to be obtained from the AKC.

Canine Good Citizen

The AKC sponsors a program to encourage dog owners to train their dogs. Local clubs perform the pass/fail tests, and dogs who pass are awarded a Canine Good Citizen Certificate. Proof of vaccination is required at the time of participation. The test includes:

1. Accepting a friendly stranger.
2. Sitting politely for petting.
3. Appearance and grooming.
4. Walking on a loose leash.
5. Walking through a crowd.
6. Sit and down on command/staying in place.
7. Come when called.
8. Reaction to another dog.
9. Reactions to distractions.
10. Supervised separation.

If more effort was made by pet owners to accomplish these exercises, fewer dogs would be cast off to the humane shelter.

OBEDIENCE

Obedience is necessary, without a doubt, but it can also become a wonderful hobby or even an obsession. Obedience classes and competition can provide wonderful companionship, not only with your dog but with your classmates or fellow competitors. It is always gratifying to discuss your dog's problems with others who have had similar experiences. The AKC acknowledged Obedience around 1936, and it has changed tremendously even though many of the exercises are basically the same.

In order to pass the Canine Good Citizen test, your Airedale must be able to get along with all kinds of people. This puppy looks like he has passed the test.

The time spent together on training helps develop a close bond between dog and owner.

Today, obedience competition is just that—very competitive. Even so, it is possible for every obedience exhibitor to come home a winner (by earning qualifying scores) even though he or she may not earn a placement in the class.

Most of the obedience titles are awarded after earning three qualifying scores (legs) in the appropriate class under three different judges. These classes offer a perfect score of 200, which is extremely rare. Each of the class exercises has its own point value. A leg is earned after receiving a score of at least

170 and at least 50 percent of the points available in each exercise. The titles are:

Companion Dog–CD
This is called the Novice Class and the exercises are:

1. Heel on leash and figure 8	40 points
2. Stand for examination	30 points
3. Heel free	40 points
4. Recall	30 points
5. Long sit–one minute	30 points
6. Long down–three minutes	30 points
Maximum total score	200 points

Companion Dog Excellent–CDX
This is the Open Class and the exercises are:

1. Heel off leash and figure 8	40 points
2. Drop on recall	30 points
3. Retrieve on flat	20 points
4. Retrieve over high jump	30 points
5. Broad jump	20 points
6. Long sit–three minutes (out of sight)	30 points
7. Long down–five minutes (out of sight)	30 points
Maximum total score	200 points

Utility Dog–UD
The Utility Class exercises are:

1. Signal Exercise	40 points
2. Scent discrimination-Article 1	30 points
3. Scent discrimination-Article 2	30 points
4. Directed retrieve	30 points

The intelligent and eager-to-please Airedale is a natural candidate for obedience work.

5. Moving stand and examination   30 points
6. Directed jumping   40 points
Maximum total score   200 points

After achieving the UD title, you may feel inclined to go after the UDX and/or OTCh. The UDX (Utility Dog Excellent) title went into effect in January 1994. It is not easily attained. The title requires qualifying simultaneously ten times in Open B and Utility B but not necessarily at consecutive shows.

The OTCh (Obedience Trial Champion) is awarded after the dog has earned his UD and then goes on to earn 100 championship points, a first place in Utility, a first place in Open and another first place in either class. The placements must be won under three different judges at all-breed obedience trials. The points are determined by the number of dogs competing in the Open B and Utility B classes. The OTCh title precedes the dog's name.

Obedience matches (AKC Sanctioned, Fun, and Show and Go) are usually available. Usually they are

Author Betty-Anne Stenmark awards Group First to Ch. Spindletop's New Kid in Town at the Westbury Kennel Association in 1998.

Performance tests help dogs apply natural instincts, like using their noses, to the show ring. Anne Sorraghan and an Airedale track a scent in the field.

sponsored by the local obedience clubs. When preparing an obedience dog for a title, you will find matches very helpful. Fun Matches and Show and Go Matches are more lenient in allowing you to make corrections in the ring. This type of training is usually very necessary for the Open and Utility Classes. AKC Sanctioned Obedience Matches do not allow corrections in the ring since they must abide by the AKC Obedience Regulations. If you are interested in showing in obedience, then you should contact the AKC for a copy of the Obedience Regulations.

TRACKING

Tracking is officially classified obedience. There are three tracking titles available: Tracking Dog (TD), Tracking Dog Excellent (TDX), Variable Surface Tracking (VST). If all three tracking titles are obtained, then the dog officially becomes a CT (Champion Tracker). The CT will go in front of the dog's name.

A TD may be earned anytime and does not have to follow the other obedience titles. There are many exhibitors that prefer tracking to obedience, and there are others who do both.

Tracking Dog–TD

A dog must be certified by an AKC tracking judge that he is ready to perform in an AKC test. The AKC can provide the names of tracking judges in your area that you can contact for

Even if you never enter a show, your Airedale can only benefit from the training you provide him.

certification. Depending on where you live, you may have to travel a distance if there is no local tracking judge. The certification track will be equivalent to a regular AKC track. A regulation track must be 440 to 500 yards long with at least two right-angle turns out in the open. The track will be aged 30 minutes to two hours. The handler has two starting flags at the beginning of the track to indicate the direction started. The dog works on a harness and 40-foot lead and must work at least 20 feet in front of the handler. An article (either a dark glove or wallet) will be dropped at the end of the track, and the dog must indicate it but not necessarily retrieve it.

People always ask what the dog tracks. Initially, the beginner on the short-aged track tracks the tracklayer. Eventually the dog learns to track the disturbed vegetation and learns to differentiate between tracks. Getting started with tracking requires reading the AKC regulations and a good book on tracking plus finding other tracking enthusiasts. Work on the buddy system. That is–lay tracks for each other so you can practice blind tracks. It is possible to train on your own, but if you are a beginner, it is a lot more entertaining to track with a buddy. It's rewarding seeing the dog use his natural ability.

Ch. Goforit Panache shows the regal stance typical of the King of Terriers.

Tracking Dog Excellent–TDX

The TDX track is 800 to 1000 yards long and is aged three to five hours. There will be five to seven turns. An article is left at the starting flag, and three other articles must be indicated on the track. There is only one flag at the start, so it is a blind start. Approximately one and a half hours after the track is laid, two tracklayers will cross over the track at two different places to test the dog's ability to stay with the original track. There will be at least two obstacles on the track such as a change of cover, fences, creeks, ditches, etc. The dog must have a TD before entering a TDX. There is no certification required for a TDX.

Variable Surface Tracking–VST

This test came into effect September 1995. The dog must

have a TD earned at least six months prior to entering this test. The track is 600 to 800 yards long and shall have a minimum of three different surfaces. Vegetation shall be included along with two areas devoid of vegetation such as concrete, asphalt, gravel, sand, hard pan, or mulch. The areas devoid of vegetation shall comprise at least one-third to one-half of the track. The track is aged three to five hours. There will be four to eight turns and four numbered articles including one leather, one plastic, one metal, and one fabric dropped on the track. There is one starting flag. The handler will work at least 10 feet from the dog.

The athletic and nimble Airedale Terrier easily succeeds in dog sports such as agility.

AGILITY

Agility was first introduced by John Varley in England at the Crufts Dog Show, February 1978, but Peter Meanwell, competitor and judge, actually developed the idea. It was officially recognized in the early '80s. Agility is extremely popular in England and Canada and growing in popularity in the US. The AKC acknowledged agility in August 1994. Dogs must be at least 12 months of age to be entered. It is a fascinating sport that the dog, handler and spectators enjoy to the utmost. Agility is a spectator sport! The dog performs off lead. The handler either runs with his dog or positions himself on the course and directs his dog with verbal and hand signals over a timed course over or through a variety of obstacles including a time out or pause. One of the main drawbacks to agility is finding a place to train. The obstacles take up a lot of space and it is very time consuming to put up and take down courses.

The titles earned at AKC agility trials are Novice Agility Dog (NAD), Open Agility Dog (OAD), Agility Dog Excellent (ADX), and Master Agility Excellent (MAX). In order to acquire an agility title, a dog must earn a qualifying score in his respective class on three separate occasions under two different judges. The MAX will be awarded after earning ten qualifying scores in the Agility Excellent Class.

PERFORMANCE TESTS

During the last decade the American Kennel Club has promoted performance tests—those events that test the

Agility is a fast-paced sport that is enjoyable for both the dogs and the spectators. Ch. Kyna's Cover Girl, OA, the first USDAA Agility Airedale, owned by Dianne Fielder.

different breeds' natural abilities. This type of event encourages a handler to devote even more time to his dog and retain the natural instincts of his breed heritage. It is an important part of the wonderful world of dogs.

Earthdog Events

For small terriers (Australian, Bedlington, Border, Cairn, Dandie Dinmont, Fox (Smooth & Wire), Lakeland, Norfolk, Norwich, Scottish, Sealyham, Skye, Welsh, West Highland White, and Dachshunds).

Limited registration (ILP) dogs are eligible and all entrants must be at least six months of age. The primary purpose of the small terriers and Dachshunds is to pursue quarry to ground, hold the game, and alert the hunter where to dig, or to bolt. There are two parts to the test: (1) the approach to the quarry and (2) working the quarry. The dog must pass both parts for a Junior Earthdog (JE). The Senior Earthdog (SE) must do a third part–to leave the den on command. The Master Earthdog (ME) is a bit more complicated.

GENERAL INFORMATION

Obedience, tracking, and agility allow the purebred dog with an Indefinite Listing Privilege (ILP) number or a limited registration to be exhibited and earn titles. Application must be made to the AKC for an ILP number.

The American Kennel Club publishes a monthly *Events* magazine that is part of the *Gazette*, their official journal for the sport of purebred dogs. The *Events* section lists upcoming shows and the secretary or superintendent for them. The majority of the conformation shows in the US are overseen by licensed superintendents. Generally, the entry closing date is approximately two-and-a-half weeks before the actual show. Point shows are fairly expensive, while the match shows cost about one third of the point show entry fee. Match shows usually take entries the day of the show but some are pre-entry. The best way to find match show information is through your local kennel club. Upon asking, the AKC can provide you with a list of superintendents, and you can write and ask to be put on their mailing lists.

Airedales can do anything! This Airedale Terrier leads his family on a cross-country skiing adventure.

Obedience trial and tracking test information is available through the AKC. Frequently these events are not superintended, but put on by the host club. Therefore you would make the entry with the event's secretary.

As you have read, there are numerous activities you can share with your dog. Regardless of what you do, it does take teamwork. Your dog can only benefit from your attention and training. We hope this chapter has enlightened you and hope, if nothing else, you will attend a show here and there. Perhaps you will start with a puppy kindergarten class, and who knows where it may lead!

HEALTH CARE

Veterinary medicine has become far more sophisticated than what was available to our ancestors. This can be attributed to the increase in household pets and consequently the demand for better care for them. Also, human medicine has become far more complex. Today diagnostic testing in veterinary medicine parallels human diagnostics. Because of better technology we can expect our pets to live healthier lives thereby increasing their life spans.

THE FIRST CHECKUP

You will want to take your new puppy/dog in for his first checkup within 48 to 72 hours after acquiring him. Many breeders strongly recommend this checkup and so do the humane shelters. A puppy/dog can appear healthy but he may have a serious problem that is not apparent to the layman. Most pets have some type of a minor flaw that may never cause a real problem.

Unfortunately if he/she should have a serious problem, you will want to consider the consequences of keeping the pet and the attachments that will be formed, which may be broken prematurely. Keep in mind there are many healthy dogs looking for good homes.

This first checkup is a good time to establish yourself with the veterinarian and learn the office policy regarding their hours and how they handle emergencies. Usually the breeder or another conscientious pet owner is a good reference for locating a capable veterinarian. You should be aware that not all veterinarians give the same quality of service. Please do not make your selection on the least expensive clinic, as they may be short changing your pet. There is the possibility that eventually it will cost you more due to improper diagnosis, treatment, etc. If you are selecting a new veterinarian, feel free to ask for a tour of the clinic. You should inquire about making an appointment for a tour since all clinics are working clinics, and therefore may not be available all day for sightseers. You may worry less if you see where your pet will be spending the day if he ever needs to be hospitalized.

THE PHYSICAL EXAM

Your veterinarian will check your pet's overall condition, which includes listening to the heart; checking the respiration; feeling the abdomen, muscles and joints; checking the mouth, which includes the gum color and signs of gum disease along with plaque buildup; checking the ears for signs of an infection or ear mites; examining the eyes; and, last but not least, checking the condition of the skin and coat.

He should ask you questions regarding your pet's eating and elimination habits and invite you to relay your questions. It is a good idea to prepare a list so as not to forget anything. He should discuss the proper diet and the quantity to be fed. If this should differ from your breeder's recommendation, then you should convey to him the breeder's choice and see if he

Four-month-old Montee has a long life ahead of him. Proper health care from the start will ensure that he will lead a full and active life.

approves. If he recommends changing the diet, then this should be done over a few days so as not to cause a gastrointestinal upset. It is customary to take in a fresh stool sample (just a small amount) for a test for intestinal parasites. It must be fresh, preferably within 12 hours, since the eggs hatch quickly and after hatching will not be observed under the microscope. If your pet isn't obliging then, usually the technician can take one in the clinic.

IMMUNIZATIONS

It is important that you take your puppy/dog's vaccination record with you on your first visit. In the case of a puppy, presumably the breeder has seen to the vaccinations up to the time you acquired custody. Veterinarians differ in their vaccination protocol. It is not unusual for your puppy to have received vaccinations for distemper, hepatitis, leptospirosis, parvovirus, and parainfluenza every two to three weeks from the age of six weeks. Usually this is a combined injection and is typically called the DHLPP. The DHLPP is given through 16 weeks of age, and it is not unusual to give another parvovirus vaccine at 18 weeks. You may wonder why so many immunizations are necessary. No one knows for sure when the puppy's maternal antibodies are gone, although it is customarily accepted that distemper antibodies are gone by 12 weeks. Usually parvovirus antibodies are gone by 16 to 18 weeks of age. However, it is possible for the maternal antibodies to be gone at a much earlier age or even a later age. Therefore immunizations are started at an early age. The vaccine will not give immunity as long as there are maternal antibodies.

The rabies vaccination is given in accordance with your local laws. A vaccine for bordetella (kennel cough) is advisable and can be given anytime from the age of five weeks. The coronavirus vaccine is not commonly given unless there is a problem locally. The Lyme vaccine is necessary in endemic areas. Lyme disease has been reported in 47 states.

Distemper

This is virtually an incurable disease. If the dog recovers, he is subject to severe nervous disorders. The virus attacks every tissue in the body and resembles a bad cold with a fever. It can cause a runny nose and eyes and cause gastrointestinal disorders, including a poor appetite, vomiting, and diarrhea. The virus is carried by raccoons, foxes, wolves, mink, and other dogs. Unvaccinated youngsters and senior citizens are very susceptible. This is still a common disease.

Hepatitis

This is a virus that is most serious in very young dogs. It is spread by contact with an infected animal or its stool or urine. The virus affects the liver and kidneys and is characterized by high fever, depression, and lack of appetite. Recovered animals may be afflicted with chronic illnesses.

Dogs can pick up diseases from other dogs. Make sure your Airedale has all his vaccinations before taking him out to play with friends.

Leptospirosis

This is a bacterial disease transmitted by contact with the urine of an infected dog, rat, or other wildlife. It produces severe symptoms of fever, depression, jaundice, and internal bleeding and was fatal before the vaccine was developed. Recovered dogs can be carriers, and the disease can be transmitted from dogs to humans.

Parvovirus

This was first noted in the late 1970s and is still a fatal disease. However, with proper vaccinations, early diagnosis and prompt treatment, it is a manageable disease. It attacks the bone marrow and intestinal tract. The symptoms include depression, loss of appetite, vomiting, diarrhea, and collapse. Immediate medical attention is of the essence.

Rabies

This is shed in the saliva and is carried by raccoons, skunks, foxes, other dogs, and cats. It attacks nerve tissue, resulting in paralysis and death. Rabies can be transmitted to people and is virtually always fatal. This disease is reappearing in the suburbs.

Bordetella (Kennel Cough)

The symptoms are coughing, sneezing, hacking, and retching accompanied by nasal discharge usually lasting from a few days to several weeks. There are several disease-producing organisms responsible for this disease. The present vaccines are helpful but do not protect for all the strains. It usually is not life threatening but in some instances it can progress to a serious bronchopneumonia. The disease is highly contagious. The vaccination should be given routinely for dogs that come in contact with other dogs, such as through boarding, training class, or visits to the groomer.

Coronavirus

This is usually self-limiting and not life threatening. It was first noted in the late '70s about a year before parvovirus. The virus produces a yellow/brown stool and there may be depression, vomiting, and diarrhea.

Lyme Disease

This was first diagnosed in the United States in 1976 in Lyme, CT in people who lived in close proximity to the deer tick. Symptoms may include acute lameness, fever, swelling of joints, and loss of appetite. Your veterinarian can advise you if you live in an endemic area.

After your puppy has completed his puppy vaccinations, you will continue to booster the DHLPP once a year. It is customary to booster the rabies one year after the first vaccine and then, depending on where you live, it should be boostered every year or every three years. This depends on your local

Bordetella attached to canine cilia. Otherwise known as kennel cough, this disease is highly contagious and should be vaccinated against routinely.

laws. The Lyme and corona vaccines are boostered annually and it is recommended that the bordetella be boostered every six to eight months.

Annual Visit

I would like to impress the importance of the annual checkup, which would include the booster vaccinations, check for intestinal parasites, and test for heartworm. Today in our very busy world it is rush,

The deer tick is the most common carrier of Lyme disease. Photo courtesy of Virbac Laboratories, Inc., Fort Worth, Texas.

rush and see "how much you can get for how little." Unbelievably, some non-veterinary businesses have entered into the vaccination business. More harm than good can come to your dog through improper vaccinations, possibly from inferior vaccines and/or the wrong schedule. More than likely you truly care about your companion dog and over the years you have devoted much time and expense to his well-being. Perhaps you are unaware that a vaccination is not just a vaccination. There is more involved. Please, please follow through with regular physical examinations. It is so important for your veterinarian to know your dog and this is especially true during middle age through the geriatric years. More than likely your older dog will require more than one physical a year. The annual physical is good preventive medicine. Through early diagnosis and subsequent treatment your dog can maintain a longer and better quality of life.

Intestinal Parasites

Hookworms

These are almost microscopic intestinal worms that can cause anemia and therefore, serious problems, including death, in young puppies. Hookworms can be transmitted to humans through penetration of the skin. Puppies may be born with them.

Roundworms

These are spaghetti-like worms that can cause a potbellied appearance and dull coat along with more severe symptoms, such as vomiting, diarrhea, and coughing. Puppies acquire these while in the mother's uterus and through lactation. Both hookworms and roundworms may be acquired through ingestion.

Whipworms

These have a three-month life cycle and are not acquired through the dam. They cause intermittent diarrhea usually with mucus. Whipworms are possibly the most difficult worm to eradicate. Their eggs are very resistant to most environmental factors and can last for years until the proper conditions enable them to mature. Whipworms are seldom seen in the stool.

Roundworm eggs, as seen on a fecal evaluation. The eggs must develop for at least 12 days before they are infectious.

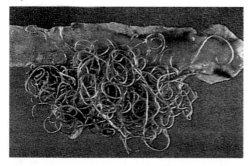

Intestinal parasites are more prevalent in some areas than others. Climate, soil, and contamination are big factors contributing to the incidence of intestinal parasites. Eggs are passed in the stool, lay on the ground, and then become infective in a certain number of days. Each of the above worms has a different life cycle. Your best chance of becoming and remaining worm-free is to always pooper-scoop your yard. A fenced-in yard keeps stray dogs out, which is certainly helpful.

I would recommend having a fecal examination on your dog twice a year or more often if there is a problem. If your dog has a positive fecal sample, then he will be given the appropriate medication and you will be asked to bring back another stool sample in a certain period of time (depending on the type of worm) and then he will be rewormed. This process goes on until he has at least two negative samples. The different types of worms

Although generally a hardy, healthy breed, the Airedale does have certain problems you must be aware of.

require different medications. You will be wasting your money and doing your dog an injustice by buying over-the-counter medication without first consulting your veterinarian.

OTHER INTERNAL PARASITES

Coccidiosis and Giardiasis

These protozoal infections usually affect puppies, especially in places where large numbers of puppies are brought

Your Airedale can pick up parasites like fleas and ticks when outdoors. Make sure to check his coat thoroughly after playing outside.

together. Older dogs may harbor these infections but do not show signs unless they are stressed. Symptoms include diarrhea, weight loss, and lack of appetite. These infections are not always apparent in the fecal examination.

Tapeworms

Seldom apparent on fecal floatation, tapeworms are diagnosed frequently as rice-like segments around the dog's anus and the base of the tail. They are long, flat, and ribbon-like, sometimes several feet in length, and made up of many segments about five-eighths of an inch long. The two most common types of tapeworm found in the dog are:
(1) First, the larval form of the flea tapeworm parasite must

mature in an intermediate host, the flea, before it can become infective. Your dog acquires this by ingesting the flea through licking and chewing.

(2) Rabbits, rodents, and certain large game animals serve as intermediate hosts for other species of tapeworm. If your dog should eat one of these infected hosts, then he can acquire tapeworms.

Dirofilaria—adult worms in the heart of a dog. Photo courtesy of Merck AgVet.

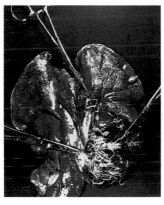

HEARTWORM DISEASE

This is a worm that resides in the heart and adjacent blood vessels of the lung that produces microfilaria, which circulate in the bloodstream. It is possible for a dog to be infected with any number of worms from one to a hundred that can be 6 to 14 inches long. It is a life-threatening disease, expensive to treat and easily prevented. Depending on where you live, your veterinarian may recommend a preventive year-round and either an annual or semiannual blood test. The most common preventive is given once a month.

EXTERNAL PARASITES

Fleas

These pests are not only the dog's worst enemy but also enemy to the owner's pocketbook. Preventing is less expensive than treating, but regardless we'd prefer to spend our money elsewhere. Likely, the majority of our dogs are allergic to the bite of a flea, and in many cases it only takes one flea bite. The protein in the flea's saliva is the culprit. Allergic dogs have a reaction, which usually results in a "hot spot." More than likely such a reaction will involve a trip to the veterinarian for treatment. Yes, prevention is less expensive. Fortunately today there are several good products available.

If there is a flea infestation, no one product is going to correct the problem. Not only will the dog require treatment

so will the environment. In general, flea collars are not very effective although there is now available an "egg" collar that will kill the eggs on the dog. Dips are the most economical but they are messy. There are some effective shampoos and treatments available through pet shops and veterinarians. An oral tablet arrived on the American market in 1995 and was popular in Europe the previous year. It sterilizes the female flea but will not kill adult fleas. Therefore the tablet, which is given monthly, will decrease the flea population but is not a "cure-all." Those dogs that suffer from flea-bite allergy will still be subjected to the bite of the flea. Another popular parasiticide is permethrin, which is applied to the back of the dog in one or two places depending on the dog's weight. This product works as a repellent causing the flea to get "hot feet" and jump off. Do not confuse this product with some of the organophosphates that are also applied to the dog's back.

Some products are not usable on young puppies. Treating fleas should be done under your veterinarian's guidance. Frequently it is necessary to combine products and the layman does not have the knowledge regarding possible toxicities. It is hard to believe but there are a few dogs that do have a natural resistance to fleas. Nevertheless it would be wise to treat all pets at the same time. Don't forget your cats. Cats just love to prowl the neighborhood and consequently return with unwanted guests.

Adult fleas live on the dog but their eggs drop off the dog into the environment. There they go through four larval stages before reaching adulthood, and thereby, are able to jump back on the poor unsuspecting dog. The cycle resumes and takes between 21 to 28 days under ideal conditions. There are environmental products available that will kill both the adult fleas and the larvae.

Ticks

After the first few weeks of life, Airedale puppies must receive vaccinations to prevent certain diseases. Your vet should put him on an immunization schedule.

Ticks carry Rocky Mountain Spotted Fever, Lyme disease, and can cause tick paralysis. They should be removed with tweezers, trying to pull out the head.

The jaws carry disease. There is a tick preventive collar that does an excellent job. The ticks automatically back out on those dogs wearing collars.

Sarcoptic Mange

This is a mite that is difficult to find on skin scrapings. The pinnal reflex is a good indicator of this disease. Rub the ends of the pinna (ear) together and the dog will start scratching with his foot. Sarcoptes are highly contagious to other dogs and to humans although they do not live long on humans. They cause intense itching.

Demodectic Mange

This is a mite that is passed from the dam to her puppies. It affects youngsters age three to ten months. Diagnosis is confirmed by skin scraping. Small areas of alopecia around the eyes, lips, and/or forelegs become visible. There is little itching unless there is a secondary bacterial infection. Some breeds are afflicted more than others.

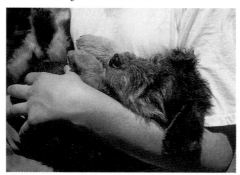

Puppies are very vulnerable and your Airedale will look to you, his owner, to take care of all his needs.

Cheyletiella

This causes intense itching and is diagnosed by skin scraping. It lives in the outer layers of the skin of dogs, cats, rabbits, and humans. Yellow-gray scales may be found on the back and the rump, top of the head, and the nose.

TO BREED OR NOT TO BREED

More than likely your breeder has requested that you have your puppy neutered or spayed. Your breeder's request is based on what is healthiest for your dog and what is most beneficial for your breed. Experienced and conscientious breeders devote many years to developing a

Annual checkups will ensure your Airedale's quality of life and help to prevent any future problems. Lily and Tucker are the picture of good health.

bloodline. In order to do this, he makes every effort to plan each breeding in regard to conformation, temperament, and health. This type of breeder does his best to perform the necessary testing (i.e., OFA, CERF, testing for inherited blood disorders, thyroid, etc.). Testing is expensive and sometimes very disheartening when a favorite dog doesn't pass his health tests. The health history pertains not only to the breeding stock but to the immediate ancestors. Reputable breeders do not want their offspring to be bred indiscriminately. Therefore you may be asked to neuter or spay your puppy. Of course there is always the exception, and your breeder may agree to let you breed your dog under his direct supervision. This is an important concept. More and more effort is being made to breed healthier dogs.

Spaying or neutering your dog will not only prevent certain diseases, but will help control the pet population.

Spay/Neuter

There are numerous benefits to performing this surgery at six months of age. Unspayed females are subject to mammary and ovarian cancer. In order to prevent mammary cancer she must be spayed prior to her first heat cycle. Later in life, an unspayed female may develop a pyometra (an infected uterus), which is definitely life threatening.

Spaying is performed under a general anesthetic and is easy on the young dog. As you might expect it is a little harder on the older dog, but that is no reason to deny her the surgery. The surgery removes the ovaries and uterus. It is important to remove all the ovarian tissue. If some is left behind, she could remain attractive to males. In order to view the ovaries, a reasonably long incision is necessary. An ovariohysterectomy is considered major surgery.

Neutering the male at a young age will inhibit some characteristic male behavior that owners frown upon. Some boys will not hike their legs and mark territory if they are neutered at six months of age. Also, neutering at a young age has hormonal benefits, lessening the chance of hormonal aggressiveness.

Surgery involves removing the testicles but leaving the scrotum. If there should be a retained testicle, then the male definitely needs to be neutered before the age of two or three years. Retained testicles can develop into cancer. Unneutered males are at risk for testicular cancer, perineal fistulas, perianal tumors and fistulas and prostatic disease.

Intact males and females are prone to housebreaking accidents. Females urinate frequently before, during, and after heat cycles, and males tend to mark territory if there is a female in heat. Males may show the same behavior if there is a visiting dog or guests.

Some breeders will sell pet-quality Airedale pups on the condition that they are spayed or neutered.

Surgery involves a sterile operating procedure equivalent to human surgery. The incision site is shaved, surgically scrubbed, and draped. The veterinarian wears a sterile surgical gown, cap, mask, and gloves. Anesthesia should be monitored by a registered technician. It is customary for the veterinarian to recommend a pre-anesthetic blood screening, looking for metabolic problems and a ECG rhythm strip to check for normal heart function. Today anesthetics are equal to human anesthetics, which enables your dog to walk out of the clinic the same day as surgery.

Some folks worry about their dog gaining weight after being neutered or spayed. This is usually not the case. It is true that some dogs may be less active so they could develop a problem, but most dogs are just as active as they were before surgery. However, if your dog should begin to gain, then you need to decrease his food and see to it that he gets a little more exercise.

DENTAL CARE for Your Dog's Life

So you've got a new puppy! You also have a new set of puppy teeth in your household. Anyone who has ever raised a puppy is abundantly aware of these new teeth. Your puppy will chew anything he can reach, chase your shoelaces, and play "tear the rag" with any piece of clothing he can find. When puppies are newly born, they have no teeth. At about four weeks of age, puppies of most breeds begin to develop their deciduous or baby teeth. They begin eating semi-solid food, fighting and biting with their littermates, and learning discipline from their mother. As their new teeth come in, they inflict more pain on their

Providing your Airedale pups with plenty of safe toys to chew on will help them keep their teeth healthy.

mother's breasts, so her feeding sessions become less frequent and shorter. By six or eight weeks, the mother will start growling to warn her pups when they are fighting too roughly or hurting her as they nurse too much with their new teeth.

Puppies need to chew. It is a necessary part of their physical and mental development. They develop muscles and necessary life skills as they drag objects around, fight over possession, and vocalize alerts and warnings. Puppies chew on things to explore their world. They are using their sense of taste to determine what is food and what is not. How else can they tell an electrical cord from a lizard? At about four months of age, most puppies begin shedding their baby teeth. Often these teeth need some help to come out and make way for the permanent teeth. The incisors (front teeth) will be replaced first. Then, the adult canine or fang teeth erupt. When the baby tooth is not shed before the permanent tooth comes in, veterinarians call it a retained deciduous tooth. This condition will often cause gum infections by trapping hair and debris between the permanent tooth and the retained baby tooth. Nylafloss® is an excellent device for puppies to use. They can toss it, drag it, and chew on the many surfaces it presents. The baby teeth can catch in the nylon material, aiding in their removal. Puppies that have adequate chew toys will have less

destructive behavior, develop more physically, and have less chance of retained deciduous teeth.

During the first year, your dog should be seen by your veterinarian at regular intervals. Your veterinarian will let you know when to bring in your puppy for vaccinations and parasite examinations. At each visit, your veterinarian should inspect the lips, teeth, and mouth as part of a complete physical examination. You should take some part in the maintenance of your dog's oral health. You should examine your dog's mouth weekly throughout his first year to make sure there are no sores, foreign objects, tooth problems, etc. If your dog drools excessively, shakes his head, or has bad breath, consult your veterinarian. By the time your dog is six months old, the permanent teeth are all in and plaque can start to accumulate on the tooth surfaces. This is when your dog needs to develop good dental-care habits to prevent calculus buildup on his teeth. Brushing is best. That is a fact that cannot be denied. However, some dogs do not like their teeth brushed regularly, or

A thorough oral inspection and teeth cleaning should be a part of your Airedale's regular grooming routine.

Chew toys, like Nylabones®, can help your Airedale exercise his teeth and gums, as well as help keep your belongings safe.

you may not be able to accomplish the task. In that case, you should consider a product that will help prevent plaque and calculus buildup.

The Plaque Attacker® and Galileo Bone® are other excellent choices for the first three years of a dog's life. Their shapes make them interesting for the dog. As the dog chews on them, the solid polyurethane massages the gums, which improves the blood circulation to the periodontal tissues. Projections on the chew devices increase the surface and are in contact with the tooth for more efficient cleaning. The unique shape and consistency prevent your dog from exerting excessive force on his own teeth or from breaking off pieces of the bone. If your dog is an aggressive chewer or weighs more than 55 pounds (25 kg), you should consider giving him a Nylabone®, the most durable chew product on the market.

The Gumabone ®, made by the Nylabone Company, is constructed of strong polyurethane, which is softer than nylon. Less powerful chewers prefer the Gumabone® to the Nylabone®. A super option for your dog is the Hercules Bone®, a uniquely shaped bone named after the great Olympian for its

exception strength. Like all Nylabone products, they are specially scented to make them attractive to your dog. Ask your veterinarian about these bones and he will validate the good doctor's prescription: Nylabones® not only give your dog a good chewing workout but also help to save your dog's teeth (and even his life, as it protects him from possible fatal periodontal diseases).

By the time dogs are four years old, 75% of them have periodontal disease. It is the most common infection in dogs. Yearly examinations by your veterinarian are essential to maintaining your dog's good health. If your veterinarian detects periodontal disease, he or she may recommend a prophylactic cleaning. To do a thorough cleaning, it will be necessary to put your dog under anesthesia. With modern gas anesthetics and monitoring equipment, the procedure is pretty safe. Your veterinarian will scale the teeth with an ultrasound scaler or hand instrument. This removes the calculus from the teeth. If there are calculus deposits below the gum line, the veterinarian will plane the roots to make them smooth. After all of the calculus has been removed, the teeth are polished with pumice in a polishing cup. If any medical or surgical treatment is needed, it is done at this time. The final step would be fluoride treatment and your follow-up treatment at home. If the periodontal disease is advanced, the veterinarian may prescribe a medicated mouth rinse or antibiotics for use at home. Make sure your dog has safe, clean, and attractive chew toys and treats. Chooz® treats are another way of using a consumable treat to help keep your dog's teeth clean.

Rawhide is the most popular of all materials for a dog to chew. This has never been good news to dog owners, because rawhide is inherently very dangerous for dogs. Thousands of dogs have died from rawhide, having swallowed the hide after it has become soft and mushy, only to cause stomach and intestinal blockage. A new rawhide product on the market has finally solved the problem of rawhide: molded Roar-Hide® from Nylabone. These are composed of processed, cut up, and melted American rawhide injected into your dog's favorite shape: a dog bone. These dog-safe devices smell and taste like rawhide but don't break

Your veterinarian should examine your Airedale's mouth, teeth, and gums as part of his annual checkup.

133

up. The ridges on the bones help to fight tartar buildup on the teeth and they last ten times longer than the usual rawhide chews.

Chew toys can also be used as rewards in training sessions. This Airedale will do anything to get his Nylabone®.

As your dog ages, professional examination and cleaning should become more frequent. The mouth should be inspected at least once a year. Your veterinarian may recommend visits every six months. In the geriatric patient, organs such as

If you give your dog good dental care during his lifetime, he will always be able to flash a healthy smile.

the heart, liver, and kidneys do not function as well as when he was young. Your veterinarian will probably want to test these organs' functions prior to using general anesthesia for dental cleaning. If your dog is a good chewer and you work closely with your veterinarian, your dog can keep all of his teeth all of his life. However, as your dog ages, his sense of smell, sight, and taste will diminish. He may not have the desire to chase, trap, or chew his toys. He will also not have the energy to chew for long periods, as arthritis and periodontal disease make chewing painful. This will leave you with more responsibility for keeping his teeth clean and healthy. The dog that would not let you brush his teeth at one year of age, may let you brush his teeth now that he is ten years old.

If you train your dog with good chewing habits as a puppy, he will have healthier teeth throughout his life.

TRAVELING with Your Dog

T he earlier you start traveling with your new puppy or dog, the better. He needs to become accustomed to traveling. However, some dogs are nervous riders and become carsick easily. It is helpful if he starts with an empty stomach. Do not despair, as it will get better if you continue taking him with you on short fun rides. How would you feel if every time you rode in the car you stopped at the doctor's for an injection? You would soon dread that nasty car. Older dogs that tend to get carsick may have more of a problem adjusting to traveling. Those dogs that are having a serious problem may benefit from some medication prescribed by the veterinarian.

When traveling with your Airedale, make sure to bring an adequate amount of food and water and make frequent stops to attend to his needs.

Do give your dog a chance to relieve himself before getting into the car. It is a good idea to be prepared for a clean up with a leash, paper towels, bag, and terry cloth towel.

The safest place for your dog is in a fiberglass crate, although close confinement can promote carsickness in some dogs. If your dog is nervous, you can try letting him ride on the seat next to you or in someone's lap.

An alternative to the crate would be to use a car harness made for dogs and/or a safety strap attached to the harness or collar. Whatever you do, do not let your dog ride in the back of a pickup truck unless he is securely tied on a very short lead. I've seen trucks stop quickly and, even though the dog was tied, he fell out and was dragged.

Another advantage of the crate is that it is a safe place to leave him if you need to run into the store. Otherwise you wouldn't be able to leave the windows down. Keep in mind

Crates are the safest way for your Airedale Terrier to travel in the car.

that while many dogs are overly protective in their crates, this may not be enough to deter dognappers. In some states it is against the law to leave a dog in the car unattended.

Never leave a dog loose in the car wearing a collar and leash. More than one dog has killed himself by hanging. Do not let him put his head out an open window. Foreign debris can be blown into his eyes. When leaving your dog unattended in a car, consider the temperature. It can take less than five minutes to reach temperatures over 100 degrees Fahrenheit.

TRIPS

Perhaps you are taking a trip. Give consideration to what is best for your dog—traveling with you or boarding. When

Because the Airedale Terrier is such an accommodating dog, he can be brought almost anywhere. traveling by car, van, or motor home, you need to think ahead about locking your vehicle. In all probability you have many valuables in the car and do not wish to leave it unlocked. Perhaps most valuable and not replaceable is your dog. Give thought to securing your vehicle and providing adequate ventilation for him. Another consideration for you when traveling with your dog is medical problems that may arise and little inconveniences, such as exposure to external parasites. Some areas of the country are quite flea infested. You may want to carry flea spray with you. This is even a good idea when staying in motels. Quite possibly you are not the only occupant of the room.

Unbelievably many motels and even hotels do allow canine guests, even some very first-class ones. Gaines Pet Foods

Corporation publishes *Touring With Towser*, a directory of domestic hotels and motels that accommodate guests with dogs. Their address is Gaines TWT, PO Box 5700, Kankakee, IL, 60902. Call ahead to any motel that you may be considering and see if they accept pets. Sometimes it is necessary to pay a deposit against room damage. The management may feel reassured if you mention that your dog will be crated. If you do travel with your dog, take along plenty of baggies so that you can clean up after him. When we all do our share in cleaning up, we make it possible for motels to continue accepting our pets. As a matter of fact, you should practice cleaning up everywhere you take your dog.

Sometimes your pet may be more comfortable left at home. A reputable pet-sitting service can take care of your Airedale's needs while you are away.

Depending on where your are traveling, you may need an up-to-date health certificate issued by your veterinarian. It is good policy to take along your dog's medical information, which would include the name, address, and phone number of your veterinarian, vaccination record, rabies certificate, and any medication he is taking.

AIR TRAVEL

When traveling by air, you need to contact the airlines to check their policy. Usually you have to make arrangements up to a couple of weeks in advance for traveling with your dog. The airlines require your dog to travel in an airline-approved fiberglass crate. Usually these can be purchased through the airlines but they are also readily available in most pet-supply stores. If your dog is not accustomed to a crate, then it is a good idea to get him acclimated to it before your trip. The day of the actual trip you should withhold water about one hour ahead of departure and food for about 12 hours. The airlines generally have temperature restrictions, which do not allow pets to travel if it is either too cold or too hot. Frequently these restrictions are based on the temperatures at the departure and arrival airports. It's best to inquire about a health certificate. These usually need to be issued within ten days of departure. You should arrange for non-stop, direct flights and if a commuter plane should be involved, check to see if it will carry dogs. Some don't. The Humane Society of the United States has put together a tip sheet for airline traveling. You can receive a copy by sending a self-addressed stamped envelope to:

The Humane Society of the United States
Tip Sheet
2100 L Street NW
Washington, DC 20037.

Regulations differ for traveling outside of the country and are sometimes changed without notice. Well in advance you need to write or call the appropriate consulate or agricultural department for instructions. Some countries have lengthy quarantines (six months). Countries also differ in their rabies vaccination requirements. For instance, it may have to be given at least 30 days ahead of your departure.

Do make sure your dog is wearing proper identification including your name, phone number, and city. You never know when you might be in an accident and separated from your dog, or your dog could be frightened and somehow manage to escape and run away.

Another suggestion would be to carry in-case-of-emergency instructions. These would include the address and phone number of a relative or friend; your veterinarian's name, address, and phone number; and your dog's medical information.

BOARDING KENNELS

Perhaps you have decided that you need to board your dog. Your veterinarian can recommend a good boarding facility or possibly a pet sitter that will come to your house. It is customary for the boarding kennel to ask for proof of vaccination for the DHLPP, rabies, and bordetella vaccine. The bordetella should have been given within six months of boarding. This is for your protection. If they do not ask for this proof, I would not board at their kennel. Ask about flea control.

Those dogs that suffer flea-bite allergy can get in trouble at a boarding kennel. Unfortunately boarding kennels are limited by how much they are able to do.

For more information on pet sitting, contact NAPPS:
National Association of Professional Pet Sitters
1200 G Street, NW
Suite 760
Washington, DC 20005.

Some pet clinics have technicians that pet sit and technicians that board clinic patients in their homes. This may be an alternative for you. Ask your veterinarian if they have an employee that can help you. There is a definite advantage to having a technician care for your dog, especially if your dog is on medication or is a senior citizen.

Airedales are happiest when able to participate in family activities. These two Airedale pups don't want to be left out of anything.

You can write for a copy of *Traveling With Your Pet* from ASPCA, Education Department, 441 E. 92nd Street, New York, NY 10128.

IDENTIFICATION and Finding the Lost Dog

There are several ways of identifying your dog. The old standby is a collar with dog license, rabies, and ID tags. Unfortunately collars have a way of being separated from the dog and tags fall off. We're not suggesting you shouldn't use a collar and tags. If they stay intact and on the dog, they are the quickest way of identification.

For several years owners have been tattooing their dogs. Some tattoos use a number with a registry. Here lies the problem because there are several registries to check. If you wish to tattoo, use your social security number. The humane shelters have the means to trace it. It is usually done on the inside of the rear thigh. The area is first shaved and numbed. There is no pain, although a few dogs do not like the buzzing sound. Occasionally, tattooing is not legible and needs to be redone.

Your Airedale should wear his collar and identification tags at all times in case he should become separated from you.

Your Airedale Terrier should be in a safe, fenced-in enclosure if left outside unsupervised. The newest method of identification is microchipping. The microchip is a computer chip that is no larger than a grain of rice. The veterinarian implants it by injection between the shoulder blades. The dog feels no discomfort. If your dog is lost and picked up by the humane society, they can trace you by scanning the microchip, which has its own code. Microchip scanners are friendly to other brands of microchips and their registries. The microchip comes with a dog tag saying the dog is microchipped. It is the safest way of identifying your dog.

FINDING THE LOST DOG

I am sure you will agree that there would be little worse than losing your dog. Responsible pet owners rarely lose their dogs. They do not let their dogs run free because they don't want harm to come to them. Not only that but in most, if not all, states there is a leash law.

Beware of fenced-in yards. They can be a hazard. Dogs find ways to escape either over or under the fence. Another fast exit is through the gate that perhaps the neighbor's child left unlocked.

Below is a list that hopefully will be of help to you if your dog is lost. Remember don't give up, keep looking. Your dog is worth your efforts.

1. Contact your neighbors and put flyers with a photo on it in their mailboxes. Information you should include would be the dog's name, breed, sex, color, age, source of identification, when your dog was last seen and where, and your name and phone numbers. It may be helpful to say the dog needs medical care. Offer a *reward*.

2. Check all local shelters daily. It is also possible for your dog to be picked up away from home and end up in an out-of-the-way shelter. Check these too. Go in person. It is not good enough to call. Most shelters are limited on the time they can hold dogs after which they are put up for adoption or euthanized. There is the possibility that your dog will not make it to the shelter for several days. Your dog could have been wandering or someone may have tried to keep him.

3. Notify all local veterinarians. Call and send flyers.

4. Call your breeder. Frequently breeders are contacted when one of their breed is found.

5. Contact the rescue group for your breed.

6. Contact local schools—children may have seen your dog.

Airedales can be very persistent in obtaining their goals. Leave your Airedale in a secure place at all times.

7. Post flyers at the schools, groceries, gas stations, convenience stores, veterinary clinics, groomers, and any other place that will allow them.

8. Advertise in the newspaper.

9. Advertise on the radio.

BEHAVIOR and Canine Communication

Studies of the human/animal bond point out the importance of the unique relationships that exist between people and their pets. Those of us who share our lives with pets understand the special part they play through companionship, service, and protection. For many, the pet/owner bond goes beyond simple companionship; pets are often considered members of the family. A leading pet food manufacturer recently conducted a nationwide survey of pet owners to gauge just how important pets were in their lives. Here's what they found:

- 76 percent allow their pets to sleep on their beds
- 78 percent think of their pets as their children
- 84 percent display photos of their pets, mostly in their homes
- 84 percent think that their pets react to their own emotions
- 100 percent talk to their pets
- 97 percent think that their pets understand what they're saying

Many people thrive on the companionship that an Airedale Terrier can provide, and owning a dog has been known to reduce stress and improve quality of life.

Are you surprised?

Senior citizens show more concern for their own eating habits when they have the responsibility of feeding a dog. Seeing that their dog is routinely exercised encourages the owner to think of schedules that otherwise may seem unimportant to the senior citizen. The older owner may be arthritic and feeling poorly but with responsibility for his dog he has a reason to get up and get moving. It is a big plus if his dog is an attention seeker who will demand such from his owner.

Over the last couple of decades, it has been shown that pets relieve the stress of those who lead busy lives. Owning a pet has been known to lessen the occurrence of heart attack and stroke.

Many single folks thrive on the companionship of a dog. Lifestyles are very different from a long time ago, and today

more individuals seek the single life. However, they receive fulfillment from owning a dog.

Most likely the majority of our dogs live in family environments. The companionship they provide is well worth the effort involved. In my opinion, every child should have the opportunity to have a family dog. Dogs teach responsibility through understanding their care, feelings, and even respecting their life cycles. Frequently those children who have not been exposed to dogs grow up afraid of dogs, which isn't good. Dogs sense timidity and some will take advantage of the situation.

Today more dogs are serving as service dogs. Since the origination of Seeing Eye dogs years ago, we now have trained hearing dogs. Also, dogs are trained to provide service for the handicapped and are able to perform many different tasks for their owners. Search and Rescue dogs, with their handlers, are sent throughout the world to assist in the recovery of disaster victims. They are lifesavers.

Your pup will have a good start in life if his parents are healthy and well adjusted.

Therapy dogs are very popular with nursing homes, and some hospitals even allow them to visit. The inhabitants truly look forward to their visits. They wanted and were allowed to have visiting dogs in their beds to hold and love.

Nationally there is a Pet Awareness Week to educate students and others about the value and basic care of our pets. Many countries take an even greater interest in their pets than Americans do. In those countries the pets are allowed to accompany their owners into restaurants and shops, etc. In the US this freedom is only available to our service dogs. Even so, we think very highly of the human/animal bond.

CANINE BEHAVIOR

Canine behavior problems are the number-one reason for pet owners to dispose of their dogs, either through new

Dog ownership can help teach a child responsibility, love, and respect for animals and can provide a child with a playmate that can match his energy level.

homes, humane shelters, or euthanasia. Unfortunately there are too many owners who are unwilling to devote the necessary time to properly train their dogs. On the other hand, there are those who not only are concerned about inherited health problems but are also aware of the dog's mental stability.

You may realize that a breed and its group relatives (i.e., sporting, hounds, etc.) show tendencies toward behavioral characteristics. An experienced breeder can acquaint you with his breed's personality. Unfortunately many breeds are labeled with poor temperaments when actually the breed as a whole is not affected, only a small percentage of individuals within the breed.

Inheritance and environment contribute to the dog's behavior. Some naïve people suggest inbreeding as the cause of bad temperaments. Inbreeding only results in poor behavior if the ancestors carry the trait. If there are excellent temperaments behind the dogs, then inbreeding will promote good temperaments in the offspring. Did you ever consider that inbreeding is what sets the characteristics of a breed? A purebred dog is the end result of inbreeding. This does not spare the mixed-breed dog from the same problems. Mixed-breed dogs frequently are the offspring of purebred dogs.

Not too many decades ago most of our dogs led a different lifestyle than what is prevalent today. Usually mom stayed home so the dog had human companionship and someone to discipline him if needed. Not much was expected from the dog. Today's mom works and everyone's life is at a much faster pace.

The dog may have to adjust to being a "weekend" dog. The family is gone all day during the week, and the dog is left to his own devices for entertainment. Some dogs sleep all day waiting for their families to come home and others become wigwam wreckers if given the opportunity. Crates do ensure the safety of the dog and the house. However, he could become a physical and emotional cripple if he doesn't get enough exercise and attention. We still appreciate and want the companionship of our dogs although we expect more from them. In many cases we tend to forget dogs are just that—*dogs,* not human beings.

Socializing and Training

Many prospective puppy buyers lack experience regarding the proper socialization and training needed to develop the type of pet we all desire. In the first 18 months, training does take some work. It is easier to start proper training before there is a problem that needs to be corrected.

The initial work begins with the breeder. The breeder should start socializing the puppy at five to six weeks of age and cannot let up. Human socializing is critical up through 12 weeks of age and likewise important during the following months. The litter should be left together during the first few weeks but it is necessary to separate the pups by ten weeks of age. Leaving them together after that time will increase competition for litter dominance. If puppies are not socialized with people by 12 weeks of age, they will be timid in later life.

The eight- to ten-week age period is a fearful time for puppies. They need to be handled very gently around children and adults. There should be no harsh discipline during this time. Starting at 14 weeks of age, the puppy begins the juvenile period, which ends when he reaches sexual maturity around 6 to 14 months of age. During the juvenile period, he needs to be introduced to strangers (adults, children, and other dogs) on the home property. At sexual maturity he will begin to bark at strangers and become more

Socialization is very important for a well-adjusted Airedale. A well-socialized dog will be able to get along with anyone.

protective. Males start to lift their legs to urinate, but if you desire you can inhibit this behavior by walking your boy on leash away from trees, shrubs, fences, etc.

Perhaps you are thinking about an older puppy. You need to inquire about the puppy's social experience. If he has lived in a kennel, he may have a hard time adjusting to people and environmental stimuli. Assuming he has had a good social upbringing, there are advantages to an older puppy.

Training includes puppy kindergarten and a minimum of one to two basic training classes. During these classes you will learn how to dominate your youngster. This is especially important if you own a large breed of dog. It is somewhat harder, if not nearly impossible, for some owners to be the alpha figure when their dog towers over them. You will be taught how to properly restrain your dog. This concept is important. Again it puts you in the alpha position. All dogs need to be restrained many times during their lives. Believe it or not, some of our worst offenders are the eight-week-old puppies that are brought to our clinic. They need to be gently restrained for a nail trim but the way they carry on you would think we were killing them. In comparison, their vaccination is a "piece of cake." When we ask dogs to do something that is not agreeable to them, then their worst comes out. Life will be easier for your dog if you expose him at a young age to the necessities of life—proper behavior and restraint.

UNDERSTANDING THE DOG'S LANGUAGE

Most authorities agree that the dog is a descendent of the wolf. The dog and wolf have similar traits. For instance both are pack oriented and prefer not to be isolated for long periods of time. Another characteristic is that the dog, like the wolf, looks to the leader—alpha—for direction. Both the wolf and the dog communicate through body language, not only within their pack but with outsiders.

Every pack has an alpha figure. The dog looks to you, or should look to you, to be that leader. If your dog doesn't receive the proper training and guidance, he very well may replace you as alpha. This would be a serious problem and is certainly a disservice to your dog.

Eye contact is one way the alpha wolf keeps order within his pack. You are alpha so you must establish eye contact with your puppy. Obviously your puppy will have to look at you. Practice eye contact even if you need to hold his head for five to ten seconds at a time. You can give him a treat as a reward. Make sure your eye contact is gentle and not threatening. Later, if he has been naughty, it is permissible to give him a long, penetrating look. There are some older dogs that never learned eye contact as puppies and cannot accept eye contact. You should avoid eye contact with these dogs since they feel threatened and will retaliate as such.

You can often tell what your dog is thinking by watching his body language. This puppy demonstrates the play bow, which means he's ready for a good time.

BODY LANGUAGE

The play bow, when the forequarters are down and the hindquarters are elevated, is an invitation to play. Puppies play fight, which helps them learn the acceptable limits of biting. This is necessary for later in their lives. Nevertheless, an owner may be falsely reassured by the playful nature of his dog's aggression. Playful aggression toward another dog or human may be an indication of serious aggression in the future. Owners should never play fight or play tug-of-war with any dog that is inclined to be dominant.

Signs of submission are:

1. Avoids eye contact.
2. Active submission—the dog crouches down, ears back, and the tail is lowered.
3. Passive submission—the dog rolls on his side with his hindlegs in the air and frequently urinates.

Signs of dominance are:

1. Makes eye contact.
2. Stands with ears up, tail up, and the hair raised on his neck.
3. Shows dominance over another dog by standing at right angles over it.

At times, your Airedale may question your authority, but he must always know that you are in charge in the relationship.

Dominant dogs tend to behave in characteristic ways such as:

1. The dog may be unwilling to move from his place (i.e., reluctant to give up the sofa if the owner wants to sit there).

2. He may not part with toys or objects in his mouth and may show possessiveness with his food bowl.

3. He may not respond quickly to commands.

4. He may be disagreeable to grooming and dislike being petted.

Dogs are popular because of their sociable nature. Those that have contact with humans during the first 12 weeks of life regard them as a member of their own species—their pack. All dogs have the potential for both dominant and submissive behavior. Only through experience and training do they learn to whom it is appropriate to show which behavior. Not all dogs are concerned with dominance but owners need to be aware of that potential. It is wise for the owner to establish his dominance early on.

A human can express dominance or submission toward a dog in the following ways:

Mischievous puppies can get into a lot of trouble if left unsupervised. Keep your puppy confined in a safe area if you cannot be with him.

1. Meeting the dog's gaze signals dominance. Averting the gaze signals submission. If the dog growls or threatens, averting the gaze is the first avoiding action to take—it may prevent attack. It is important to establish eye contact with the puppy. The older dog that has not been exposed to eye contact may see it as a threat and will not be willing to submit.

2. Being taller than the dog signals dominance; being lower signals submission. This is why, when attempting to make friends with a strange dog or catch the runaway, one should kneel down to his level. Some owners see their dogs become dominant when allowed on the furniture or on the bed. Then he is at the owner's level.

3. An owner can gain dominance by ignoring all the dog's social initiatives. The owner pays attention to the dog only when he obeys a command.

No dog should be allowed to achieve dominant status over any adult or child. Ways of preventing this are as follows:

1. Handle the puppy gently, especially during the three- to four-month period.

2. Let the children and adults handfeed him and teach him to take food without lunging or grabbing.

3. Do not allow him to chase children or joggers.

4. Do not allow him to jump on people or mount their legs. Even females may be inclined to mount. It is not only a male habit.

5. Do not allow him to growl for any reason.

6. Don't participate in wrestling or tug-of-war games.

7. Don't physically punish a puppy for aggressive behavior. Restrain him from repeating the infraction and teach an alternative behavior. Dogs should earn everything they receive from their owners. This would include sitting to receive petting or treats, sitting before going out the door, and sitting to receive the collar and leash. These types of exercises reinforce the owner's dominance.

Young children should never be left alone with a dog. It is important that children learn some basic obedience commands so they have some control over the dog. They will gain the respect of their dog.

FEAR

One of the most common problems dogs experience is being fearful. Some dogs are more afraid than others. On the lesser side, which is sometimes humorous to watch, dogs can be afraid of a strange object. They act silly when something is out of place in the house. We call his problem perceptive intelligence. He realizes the abnormal within his known environment. He does not react the same way in strange environments since he does not know what is normal there.

On the more serious side is a fear of people. This can result in backing off, seeking his own space and saying "leave me alone" or it can result in an aggressive behavior that may lead to challenging the person. Respect that the dog wants to be left alone and give him time to come forward. If you approach the cornered dog, he may resort to snapping. If you leave him alone, he may decide to come forward, which should be rewarded with a treat.

Some dogs may initially be too fearful to take treats. In these cases it is helpful to make sure the dog hasn't eaten for about 24 hours. Being a little hungry encourages him to accept the treats, especially if they are of the "gourmet" variety.

Dogs can be afraid of numerous things, including loud noises and thunderstorms. Invariably the owner rewards the dog (by comforting) when it shows signs of fearfulness. When your dog is frightened, direct his attention to something else and act happy. Don't dwell on his fright.

AGGRESSION

Some different types of aggression are: predatory, defensive, dominance, possessive, protective, fear induced, noise provoked, "rage" syndrome (unprovoked aggression), maternal, and aggression directed toward other dogs. Aggression is the most common behavioral problem encountered. Protective breeds are expected to be more aggressive than others, but with the proper upbringing they can make very dependable companions. You need to be able to read your dog.

Problem behaviors like digging may be a sign of boredom. Make sure you give your Airedale plenty of positive outlets in which to direct his energy.

Many factors contribute to aggression including genetics and environment. An

improper environment, which may include the living conditions, lack of social life, excessive punishment, being attacked or frightened by an aggressive dog, etc., can all influence a dog's behavior. Even spoiling him and giving too much praise may be detrimental. Isolation and the lack of human contact or exposure to frequent teasing by children or adults also can ruin a good dog.

Lack of direction, fear, or confusion lead to aggression in those dogs that are so inclined. Any obedience exercise, even the sit and down, can direct the dog and help him to overcome fear and/or confusion. Every dog should learn these commands as a youngster, and there should be periodic reinforcement.

When a dog is showing signs of aggression, you should speak calmly (no screaming or hysterics) and firmly give a command that he understands, such as the sit. As soon as your dog obeys, you have assumed your dominant position. Aggression presents a problem because there may be danger to others. Sometimes it is an emotional issue. Owners may consciously or unconsciously encourage their dog's aggression. Other owners show responsibility by accepting the problem and taking measures to keep it under control. The owner is responsible for his dog's actions, and it is not wise to take a chance on someone being bitten, especially a child. Euthanasia is the solution for some owners and in severe cases this may be the best choice. However, few dogs are that dangerous and very few are that much of a threat to their owners. If caution is exercised and professional help is gained early on, most cases can be controlled.

Some authorities recommend feeding a lower protein diet (less than 20 percent). They believe this can aid in reducing aggression. If the dog loses weight, then vegetable oil can be added. Veterinarians and behaviorists are having some success with pharmacology. In many cases treatment is possible and can improve the situation.

If you have done everything according to "the book" regarding training and socializing and are still having a behavior problem, don't procrastinate. It is important that the problem gets attention before it is out of hand. It is estimated that 20 percent of a veterinarian's time may be devoted to dealing with problems before they become so intolerable that the dog is separated from his home and owner. If your veterinarian isn't able to help, he should refer you to a behaviorist.

SUGGESTED READING

TS-214
Skin & Coat Care For
Your Dog
432 pages, over 300
full-color photos

TS-249
Owner's Guide to Dog
Health
224 pages, over 190
full-color photos

JG-109
A New Owner's Guide
to Training the Perfect
Puppy
160 pages, 150 full-
color photos

TS-258
Training Your Dog for
Sports and Other Activities
160 pages, over 200 full-
color photos

INDEX